THE BIBLE

¶ The Gospell off
Sancte Jhon.

The fyrst Chapter.

In the begynn
was that worde/ã
worde was with god: a
was thatt worde, The
was in the begynnynge
god. All thyngf were m,
it/ and with out it was
noo thige/ that made wa
it was lyfe/ And lyfe w
light of mē/ And the ligh
neth i darcknes/ ād darcknes cōprehēded
There was a mā sent from god/ whose
was Jhon. The same cã as a witnes/ tc
witnes oftheligt/ that all men thzough
ghtbeleve. He was nott that light: but to
witnes of the light. That was ã true ligt
whlightenth all men that cam/ ito the w

The Bible

Michael Keene

LION
ACCESS
GUIDES

Published by
Lion Publishing plc
Mayfield House, 256 Banbury Road,
Oxford OX2 7DH, England
www.lion-publishing.co.uk
ISBN 0 7459 5065 5

First edition 2002
10 9 8 7 6 5 4 3 2 1 0

Typeset in 10.25/11 Venetian 301
Printed and bound in China

Text acknowledgments
Scripture quotations taken from the *Holy
Bible, New International Version*, copyright ©
1973, 1978, 1984 by International Bible
Society. Used by permission of Hodder &
Stoughton Limited. All rights reserved.
'NIV' is a registered trademark of
International Bible Society. UK trademark
number 1448790.
Revised English Bible with the Apocrypha
copyright © 1989 by Oxford University
Press and Cambridge University Press.

Picture acknowledgments
Please see page 160.

Contents

Note
Throughout this
series the convention
is followed of dating
events by the
abbreviations BCE
(Before Common Era)
and CE (Common
Era). They correspond
precisely to the more
familiar BC and AD.

Introducing the Bible

The Bible is the foundation stone of two religions, Judaism and Christianity, and is one of the great classics of world literature. It was written many centuries ago, yet millions of people across the globe still read it enthusiastically today.

The Old and New Testaments
The first part of the Bible (the entire Hebrew Bible for Judaism, the Old Testament for Christianity) charts one of the most remarkable stories in history – the history of the Jewish people over the centuries, from their small and insignificant beginnings, through their many hopes and disappointments, to times when even their very existence was in doubt. The second part of the Bible, the New Testament, follows the early years of the Christian faith, from its roots in the life and teachings of Jesus of Nazareth, to the origins and growth of the early Christian Church in the middle of the first century CE.

Making the Bible available
The influence of the Bible has been incalculable. It contains some of the world's most beautiful poetry, poignant narratives and memorable characters. Its influence upon Western art and literature has stretched well beyond the purely religious. The Bible

is the most widely translated, printed, distributed and bestselling book of all time. Complete books of the Bible have now been translated into more than 2,000 languages and dialects – and the work of translation still continues. The complete Bible is now available in well over 300 languages, with the New Testament alone circulating in over 600 languages. In the modern world nine out of every ten people have ready access to the Bible.

The Bible has also inspired social movements across the world. In 19th-century Britain, for example, William Wilberforce was encouraged by what he read in the Bible to launch a campaign against slavery. In the mid-20th century Martin Luther King, Jr, based his challenge to American civil rights and race relations upon what he knew of the Bible and its message. At the end of the 20th century church groups in South Africa, inspired by the Bible, were instrumental in bringing about the collapse of apartheid and an end to the segregation of races.

This Access Guide begins with an outline of Bible history and a portrayal of the world of the Bible, then shows how the Bible was put together and translated into many languages. Next we explore the main contents of the Bible, and examine how the different books of the Old and New Testaments were produced by different writers, using different styles of writing and addressing different audiences. Then we look at the Bible in contemporary times and see how it has influenced – and been influenced by – the world in which we live.

The Bible concentrates on two main stories: the story of Israel and the story of Jesus.

Israel's earliest ancestors inhabited a world of tiny walled cities and kingdoms. These strongholds protected the settlers who farmed the lands, but there was still a constant threat from nomadic tribes in search of good grazing for their animals.

First Abraham, then Isaac and Jacob, became the patriarchs of the growing Israelite nation, which soon found itself undergoing more than 400 years of slavery in Egypt. When the Israelites finally escaped they were inspired by their faith in God to search for the Promised Land of Canaan, led first by Moses and then by Joshua.

For a long time Israel was little more than a loose coalition of different tribes under their own leaders, or 'judges'. These tribes found it hard to defend themselves against powerful enemies, so the people demanded a king to help protect them. Saul, the first monarch, was succeeded by David and then Solomon. After Solomon's death, however, the nation split into the two kingdoms of Israel and Judah. Israel survived until 721 BCE when it was overrun by the Assyrians. Then, in 586 BCE, Judah was overwhelmed by the Babylonians, who

Sunrise from Mount Sinai, where God gave Moses details of the Law.

destroyed Jerusalem and forced the majority of the population into exile.

After the Babylonian invasion the land of Palestine (Israel and Judah) was occupied by the Persians and then the Romans. While the country was under Roman control, Jesus was born in the small village of Bethlehem. Jesus spoke of the kingdom of God, which was offered to the poor, the needy and the socially excluded. Jesus' enemies eventually brought about his death, but three days later he returned to life. Shortly afterwards God empowered the first Christian believers with his Holy Spirit and the Church was born.

God's richness is such that he can totally give himself to every man, can be there only for him — and likewise for a second and third, for millions and thousands of millions. That is the mystery of his infinity and inexhaustible richness.

LADISLAUS BOROS,
20TH-CENTURY PROTESTANT THEOLOGIAN

OVERVIEW OF BIBLE HISTORY

Contents

The Patriarchs

The patriarchs were the principal ancestors of the Israelites. The nation of Israel grew from the children of these 'father figures'.

The available archaeological evidence places the patriarchs of Israel – Abraham, Isaac and Jacob – within the culture of Mesopotamia, sometime between 2000 BCE and 1200 BCE. The stories of the patriarchs found in Genesis are often called the patriarchal narratives because these individuals laid the foundation for the subsequent history of the nation.

Abraham

Jews look on Abraham as the principal recipient of the promises God gave to his people and this makes him the recognized 'father of the Jewish nation'. Abraham, or Abram as he was originally called, lived during the early centuries of the second millennium BCE, during the Middle Bronze Age. When God called Abraham he promised him a land of many descendants and a great name, and prophesied that Abraham would become a blessing to many people.

Abraham and his wife Sarah were very old when these promises were made and well beyond normal childbearing age. Nevertheless, they conceived a child and Sarah gave birth to their son Isaac. They attributed this incredible event to the grace and power of God, but the ultimate test of Abraham's faith was when God ordered him to make a human sacrifice of Isaac. Abraham's faith and conviction that God would instead provide another suitable sacrifice and spare Isaac made him the Bible's supreme example of trust in God.

Isaac

Isaac was Abraham's and Sarah's promised son. His name means 'he laughs' and reflects his

A group of votive statuettes carved from limestone, alabaster and gypsum. They were found in a Sumerian temple and could be nearly 5,000 years old. They would have been part of a culture similar to that from which Abraham came.

The nomadic lifestyle of the patriarchs would not have differed much from that of present-day Bedouins.

parents' incredulity at God's announcement of his birth. Isaac himself is a somewhat shadowy figure in the Old Testament between Abraham and Jacob. He wins most respect in his most passive moments – when he was a potential sacrifice and when a wife was found for him.

Jacob

Through his 12 sons Jacob was the ancestor of the 12 tribes of Israel, which were the foundation of the nation. Much of his life was plagued with family problems: he tricked his brother Esau out of his birthright, and showed favouritism towards his two youngest sons, Joseph and Benjamin. Jacob died in Egypt but was buried in the Promised Land of Canaan as a final recognition of his faith in God.

God's promise to Abraham that he would be the father of a great nation began to be fulfilled through Jacob.

The Lord had said to Abram,
'Leave your country, your people
and your father's household and
go to the land I will show you.
I will make you into a great nation
and I will bless you;
I will make your name great,
and you will be a blessing.
I will bless those who bless you,
and whoever curses you I will curse;
and all peoples on earth
will be blessed through you.'

GENESIS 12:1–3

From Exodus to Promised Land

The exodus took place when the Israelites escaped from slavery in Egypt and spent the next 40 years travelling through the desert to their Promised Land of Canaan.

Jacob's descendants lived in Egypt for more than 450 years, during which time they became the nation of Israel. The rulers of Egypt began to feel threatened by this growing band of people and tightened their grip on them. They put the Israelites to work as slaves in the cornfields and on various building projects. To keep their numbers down they drowned many Jewish newborn babies in the River Nile.

Moses

Early in the 13th century BCE God inspired Moses to lead the Israelites out of slavery to the Promised Land of Canaan. With his brother Aaron lending moral support, Moses repeatedly asked the Pharaoh of Egypt to set the Israelites free, but it took a series of 10 plagues of increasing severity to finally persuade him to act. The last plague, which caused the death of the first-born child in every Egyptian household, was the deciding factor. Although the Pharaoh changed his mind afterwards and gave chase, the miraculous parting of the waters of the Reed Sea (not the Red Sea) allowed the Israelites to pass through to safety. This dash for freedom, known as the exodus, has been celebrated by Jews ever since in their annual Passover festival.

As described in the Bible the exodus is the supreme moment in Jewish history, when God delivered his people from slavery and established the nation of Israel in a land of its own. The Bible also makes it clear that it was God alone who subdued the

When Moses went up on the mountain, the cloud covered it, and the glory of the Lord settled on Mount Sinai. For six days the cloud covered the mountain, and on the seventh day the Lord called to Moses from within the cloud. To the Israelites the glory of the Lord looked like a consuming fire on top of the mountain. Then Moses entered the cloud as he went on up the mountain. And he stayed on the mountain 40 days and 40 nights.

EXODUS 24:15–18

Egyptians; Moses is cast as a rather reluctant human accessory, although he displays great courage on occasions. The exodus became the pattern for later mighty acts of God.

The Ten Commandments

After travelling through the desert for three months the Israelites camped at the foot

God's relationship with his people, while the last six deal with basic human relationships within a religious community. Jesus accepted the importance of this Law, but stressed that it applied to people's motives as well as their deeds.

Moses led the Israelites to the verge of the Promised Land, but it was Joshua, his successor,

Luxor temple, Egypt. At first a sanctuary for Abraham's descendants, by the time of Moses, Egypt had become an oppressive regime whose only use for the Hebrews was as slaves to develop their ambitious building projects.

of Mount Sinai. There God made an agreement known as a 'covenant', in which he promised that the Israelites would remain his people as long as they kept his Law. This Law, including the Ten Commandments, was set out in the Torah (the first five books of the Old Testament). These were inscribed on two stone tablets and are usually called the 'Ten Words' or the Decalogue by Jews. The first four commandments outline

who actually took them across the River Jordan into their new home. Joshua defeated the kings of the Canaanite city-states, but the Israelites never completed their conquest of the land. There would always be enemies to harass them in the decades to come.

The Judges

After the 12 tribes settled in Canaan they were led by different 'judges', men and women chosen by God to help a disparate people deal with various military challenges.

The book of Judges in the Old Testament deals with the fortunes of the 12 Israelite tribes in Canaan before they were unified under the leadership of a king. The tribes had pledged themselves to the worship of Yahweh (God) alone, but after the death of Joshua they began to give their allegiance to the many nature deities of Canaan. As a result, the Israelites fell under God's judgment, but each time they repented and God chose a judge to prevent it happening again. This cycle of repentance and failure was repeated many times until the appearance of the last judge, Samuel, led to the formation of a new system of government – a monarchy.

The book of Judges

The book of Judges tells the story of 12 heroes and heroines, all of whom were local figures who became national symbols. Although each judge is represented as the ruler of the entire Israelite nation they were actually leaders of individual tribes.

The first story-cycle

Standing stones were set up on sites of religious significance all over the ancient Near East. The 10 monoliths of the Canaanite 'high place' at Gezer date from around 1600 BCE.

concerns the exploits of Ehud, who assassinated King Eglon of Moab, the oppressor of the Israelites. The next narrative concerns the military campaign of the prophetess Deborah. This is most notable for the song of triumph that Deborah sings, which describes how even the stars and the torrential waters of the river are believed to have assisted in the victory.

Another narrative tells the story of Gideon. This is followed by the account of Jephthah which mixes historical description with folklore themes — the lowly birth of Jephthah and the sacrifice of the judge's virgin daughter, the

result of an ill-judged and tragic vow. The sacrifice is said to have led to the introduction of an annual festival of lament.

A final narrative concerns the well-known story of Samson whose birth is reminiscent of Isaac's: a childless woman is given a divine promise that she will conceive. Unlike the other judges Samson's greatness is announced before his birth. He inflicts defeat on Israel's great enemy, the Philistines, through extraordinary feats of strength, including the slaying of 1,000 men with the jawbone of an ass. His lover, Delilah, discovers the source of his strength and disempowers him by cutting off his hair, but he regains his strength for long enough to demolish a Philistine temple, killing everyone inside, including himself.

A pottery cult mask found at Hazor, thought to have been connected with the worship of Baal.

The book of Judges describes Israel during the time of the judges thus: 'In those days there was no king in Israel; all the people did what was right in their own eyes.' However, things hardly improved even when there was a whole succession of kings in Israel.

GIDEON

A local folk-hero, Gideon upheld the social institution of the blood-feud by killing the two kings of Midian who had slaughtered his brothers. He rose from obscurity to prominence by leading his tribe in battle, with the result that the Israelites wanted to make him their king, an offer he refused. His fitness for leadership is demonstrated by his initial reluctance to take command, his hatred of idolatry and his courageous faith. Later, however, he did compromise with pagan idolatry.

Israel's First Kings

When Samuel, the last of the judges, grew old the people demanded a king to rule over them like the other nations. Samuel warned them that a monarchy would lead to army conscription, forced labour and oppression, but the people persisted in their demand. Samuel did as they asked.

The first king of Israel, Saul, was drawn from the smallest of the tribes, the tribe of Benjamin, in order to minimize inter-tribal rivalry – a frequent problem in early Israel.

Saul

Saul was appointed king around 1050 BCE and fought a successful battle against the Ammonites. The Philistines became a constant thorn in his flesh. Although Saul was allowed to remain on the throne of Israel, God turned his back on him and the spotlight fell on a young man named David instead. Saul was increasingly troubled by depression and was later killed in battle by the Philistines. Saul is one of the saddest figures in the Bible: his desperate later life showed the dire consequences of rejecting God's command.

David's experience of killing a bear and a lion while guarding his father's sheep gave him confidence that God would also enable him to overcome the Philistine Goliath. *David Killing a Bear* by the Master of Mary of Burgundy from a Book of Hours, c. 1470–90.

David

David, Israel's greatest king and the ancestor of Jesus, ruled from 1000 BCE to 951 BCE. His military conquests led to the establishment of Israel's only empire.

After capturing the city of Jerusalem from the Jebusites he made it the capital of his empire and united the different tribes under his leadership. He strengthened this unity by restoring the Ark of the Covenant, a golden box containing the tablets on which the Ten Commandments were inscribed, to the heart of religious life in Jerusalem. This Ark was a precious symbol of God's presence with Israel.

It was customary for men to have more than one wife and Solomon married many foreign women to secure Israel's trade contacts and treaties. According to the biblical record he had 700 wives and 300 concubines! Such close links with other nations involved, among other things, the importation of many foreign deities into Israel, and weakened Israel's allegiance to God.

SOLOMON

David's son and successor ruled Israel between 961 BCE and 922 BCE, during which time Israel enjoyed unrivalled prosperity and peace. Solomon's wealth was largely based on trade, but his greatest achievement was in building, mainly concentrated on Jerusalem. His taxation and conscription policies were unpopular and he allowed his extensive harem to introduce pagan practices into the country. As a punishment, God pronounced that Solomon's kingdom would be divided into two, an event which happened within months of the king's death. Solomon acquired a reputation for wisdom and the book of Proverbs is traditionally ascribed to him.

The legendary wisdom of Solomon was displayed in his judgment concerning the disputed parentage of a baby. The scene is depicted here in a 14th-century English psalter.

God's covenant promise to David was of an eternal dynasty and empire. Through him God promised to build two 'houses', one in the form of a dynasty and the other in the form of the Temple (the house of God) which was built in Jerusalem by David's son and successor, Solomon.

David's achievements were considerable. He transformed Israel from a disjointed collection of tribes into a single empire incorporating the territories of Philistia and Moab. As a gifted musician he is traditionally thought to have contributed to the book of Psalms. The Bible, though, also highlights David's weaknesses: his adultery with Bathsheba; his scheme to have her husband, Uriah, killed; and his doting over-indulgence of his sons. This last weakness was to cost Israel dearly in the future.

The Divided Kingdom

Soon after Solomon's death the nation of Israel was divided into two kingdoms: Israel in the north and Judah in the south. In Israel the prophets Elijah and Elisha tried to restore true faith to the people.

The division of the kingdom: Israel and Judah and the surrounding nations.

Under the leadership of Solomon Israel had become a rich and powerful empire, but the people were burdened with heavy taxes and forced labour. When Solomon's son Rehoboam succeeded his father in 930 BCE the people rebelled against his authority and the nation was split into two.

The two kingdoms

The kingdom of Judah, made up of the two tribes of Judah and Benjamin, was small. Rehoboam continued to rule this kingdom from Jerusalem. The kingdom of Israel comprised the remaining 10 tribes and Jeroboam I was its first king. Israel was ruled from Shechem, with new centres of worship set up at Dan and Bethel, as the new kingdom was cut off from the Temple in Jerusalem.

Several kings of Judah tried to extend their authority over Israel but were unsuccessful. Eventually King Jehoshaphat of Judah formed an alliance with King Ahab of Israel to unite against any enemy that

The kingdom of Judah was only about a third of the size of the kingdom of Israel, measuring some 5,630 square kilometres in area.

threatened their two countries. In the biblical record the kings of Israel and Judah are simply classified as 'good' or 'bad' depending on whether or not they tried to prevent pagan deities from being worshipped in their country. Uzziah and Hezekiah of Judah are singled out for praise on this basis, while Ahab of Israel is condemned as one of the worst.

Elijah and Elisha

During the years following the division of the nation two prophets spoke out for the pure worship of God in Israel. The first, Elijah, took his stand against King Ahab and the worship of the Caananite deity, Baal, in the northern kingdom in the ninth century BCE. He successfully challenged the 400 priests of Baal to a contest at Mount Carmel to show the people that Yahweh was the one true God. Elijah was persecuted by Ahab's wife,

Jezebel, but God protected him and the untimely deaths of both Ahab and Jezebel, which he had prophesied, fully vindicated him. Elijah's ministry resulted in the preservation of a faithful remnant of people who worshipped God. As a reward for his faithfulness he did not experience death; rather he was taken up into heaven in a whirlwind at the end of his life – a biblical precedent for the ascension of Jesus into heaven.

Elisha was Elijah's protégé as the leading prophet in the latter half of the ninth century BCE. He prophesied in Israel for more than 50 years and pointed to the vivid contrast between true faith and the unbelief of Israel's kings. He spoke about God's sovereignty over all the nations and brought about the healing of Naaman, a Syrian general, from leprosy.

The remains of a pillared building, probably stables or a storehouse, at Hazor. The city was of strategic importance and was destroyed by Joshua in his conquest of Canaan. It was rebuilt and fortified under Solomon and later Omri and Ahab.

19

The Assyrians

Both Judah and Israel were very vulnerable and had only been safe during the reigns of David and Solomon because there was no powerful adversary in the region. All that changed, however, when Assyria attained a seemingly impregnable position of power.

Assyria was a country in northern Mesopotamia (modern Iraq) that established an all-powerful empire in the eighth and seventh centuries BCE. This new power was based on the might of the infamously cruel Assyrian army, although the Assyrians were also a highly cultured people who produced outstanding literature, art and architecture.

Subduing Israel and Judah

From the middle of the ninth century BCE, the time of King

THE DESTRUCTION OF ISRAEL

King Hoshea of Israel rebelled against the Assyrians and refused to pay the yearly tribute, so King Shalmanesar V began a three-year siege of Samaria, the capital of Israel, until it fell. The Israelites were exiled to Assyria and the northern kingdom of Israel was destroyed in 722/721 BCE. The 10 tribes of Israel, whose homeland it was, were never to be heard of again.

Soon after the destruction of Israel the Assyrians defeated Egypt. Then, in 701 BCE, the powerful King Sennacherib besieged Jerusalem because King Hezekiah of Judah stopped paying him tribute. The Bible records that Hezekiah trusted in God and the city of Jerusalem was saved from the enemy. Sennacherib returned to Assyria, where he was murdered by two of his sons.

Sargon II, the Assyrian king who completed the three-year siege of Samaria, in consultation, possibly with his son and successor, Sennacherib. The relief, dating from around 710 BCE, was found at Sargon's splendid capital at Khorsabad.

The Bible is clear that Assyria was destroyed because of its godlessness. Nevertheless, it is also apparent that Assyria's invasion of Judah and Israel was permitted by God as a punishment for the disobedience of both countries.

Ahab in Israel, the kings of Assyria repeatedly attacked Israel. Shalmanesar III of Assyria exacted an annual tribute from King Jehu of Israel (841–814 BCE). Later, Ahaz, king of Judah (735–715 BCE), asked Tiglath Pileser III of Assyria to help him fight Syria and Israel. The king of Assyria agreed and defeated them both, but Judah had to accept Assyrian sovereignty over the country as a consequence.

The Assyrian empire

The Assyrian empire was at the height of its awesome power between about 880 BCE and 612 BCE. It was based on the three cities of Asshur, Calah and Nineveh. It controlled not only Israel and Judah, but also Egypt, Syria and Babylonia. However, the empire eventually grew too unwieldy and conquered countries began to regain their independence. In 612 BCE the capital city of Nineveh was destroyed by the Medes and Persians.

The Babylonians

The early sixth century BCE saw the greatest possible challenge to the Jewish people. Many of them were forced to rebuild their lives in a foreign country when they were taken off into Babylonian exile.

The Babylonians conquered Nineveh in 612 BCE, ending more than two centuries of Assyrian domination. Then, a decade after Jehoiachin became king of Judah in 597 BCE, the Babylonians conquered Jerusalem. Babylonian policy was to take the leading members of a conquered people into exile in order to weaken any resistance to their control.

The fall of Jerusalem

In 587 BCE Zedekiah, a puppet king placed on the throne of Judah by Nebuchadnezzar of Babylon, appealed to Egypt for military help. For 18 months the Babylonians laid siege to the city of Jerusalem until it was captured; a humiliated Zedekiah was blinded and led into captivity in chains. Valuable objects, including many treasures from Jerusalem's Temple complex, were plundered and the inhabitants of the capital city taken with their king into exile. Only the very poor were left behind, without any leadership, to cultivate the land.

The fate of the exiles

Little is known about the immediate fate of the exiles. The majority of people were probably put to work tilling the land or working on the various irrigation projects which made the grain fields of Mesopotamia so fertile. The fact that the majority of exiles were permitted to live together encouraged them to retain a sense of national

> *This is what the Lord Almighty, the God of Israel, says to all those I carried into exile from Jerusalem to Babylon: 'Build houses and settle down; plant gardens and eat what they produce. Marry and have sons and daughters; find wives for your sons and give your daughters in marriage… Increase in number there; do not decrease. Also, seek the peace and prosperity of the city to which I have carried you into exile. Pray to the Lord for it, because if it prospers, you too will prosper.*
>
> JEREMIAH 29:4–7

identity and pride. It also gave them some measure of control over their own local social and religious affairs.

Religious life was nevertheless very different for the exiles. Without the Temple

and the dietary laws. The written records of God's goodness in the past, especially the Torah, were valued more highly than ever. Instead of allowing the exiles to wallow in nostalgia, the prophets encouraged them to put down roots in Babylon and many did just that. They farmed, became successful in business or entered royal service. These roots grew so strong that when the opportunity came for the people to return to their homeland many of them decided to remain in Babylon. Meanwhile, for other exiles, the dream of returning home continued to inspire them with hope.

Very little remains today of the splendour of ancient Babylon. This glazed brick relief of a lion once formed part of the Marduk Processional Way to the Ishtar Gate, which was built during the reign of Nebuchadnezzar II (605–562 BCE).

in Jerusalem they were dependent on the prophets Ezekiel, Isaiah and Jeremiah to help them understand the will of God in their new situation. They were denied the religious security provided by the Temple and its sacrifices. Instead, emphasis was placed on those aspects of their religion which could be observed anywhere: keeping the Sabbath day, circumcision

Return from Exile

The Babylonian empire was superseded by that of Persia in the sixth century BCE and the Jews were encouraged to return to their homeland under the leadership of Ezra and Nehemiah. Some did and they rebuilt the walls of Jerusalem; others chose to remain in permanent exile.

The book of Ezra opens with a decree from King Cyrus the Great of Persia, following his capture of Babylon in 539 BCE. He attributes his military victories to Yahweh, 'the God of heaven', and states that Yahweh 'has charged me to build him a house in Jerusalem'. This was the second Temple, to replace the one built by Solomon, and he authorized the return of the exiles to begin this work. Ezra informs us that, following the king's decree, a caravan of deportees returned to Judah, about 50,000 people in all. It seems likely that they drifted back gradually rather than all at once.

Rebuilding the Temple

It was during the reign of Artaxerxes I of Persia (464–423 BCE) that Ezra and Nehemiah came to Jerusalem. Ezra, a priest, discovered that many men who had remained in Jerusalem during the exile had married foreign wives. He found this deeply disturbing and called on them to return to the true faith and, if necessary, leave their wives and children. Nehemiah, who had been the wine steward of Artaxerxes in Susa, returned to Jerusalem to begin the work of rebuilding the city walls. He organized the work by allocating specific sections of the wall to different families and the reconstruction was finished amid general rejoicing within 52 days.

Cyrus the Great of Persia built a vast network of highways – 2,735 kilometres in length – to link up his immense empire. It took his envoys a month to ride the full circuit, collecting remounts at 111 staging posts on the way.

A relief of a Mede leading two horses from the palace of the Assyrian king Sargon II at Khorsabad.

THE JEWISH DISPERSION

After the exile many Jews did not return to Jerusalem. They remained in different parts of the Persian empire where they had put down roots. This 'dispersion' of the Jewish people (called the 'Diaspora') became a significant factor in New Testament times. One important consequence was that, because of their separation from the Temple in Jerusalem, the Jews of the Diaspora built their religious life around the local synagogue instead. These places became important centres of learning and worship, and this was significant for the rapid spread of Jewish communities throughout the Mediterranean world in the centuries ahead.

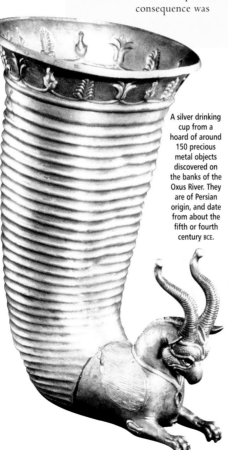

A silver drinking cup from a hoard of around 150 precious metal objects discovered on the banks of the Oxus River. They are of Persian origin, and date from about the fifth or fourth century BCE.

The new community

For 12 years Nehemiah was the governor of Judah, appointed by the Persians. He and Ezra introduced many changes to bring daily religious and social life into line with the teachings of the Torah. Nehemiah took steps to prevent wealthy Jews from over-charging their poor neighbours for food, while Ezra read and explained God's Law, the Torah, to the people. The Jewish people gave their assent to a document signed by Ezra and Nehemiah which solemnly promised that they would obey all the commands and laws of God in future.

The Greek and Roman Empires

The story told in the Old Testament ends with the rebuilding of the Temple and city walls in Jerusalem. There is then a gap before the New Testament story begins. During this time the Persian and Greek empires came and went, before the Romans began to exert their iron grip on the ancient world.

In 333 BCE Alexander the Great of Macedon routed the huge army of Darius III at the battle of Issus, burned the city of Persepolis and absorbed the Persian empire into his own. Alexander extended his empire as far as India, founding Greek city-states wherever he went. He believed passionately in Greek ideals and culture and sought to establish its thought and architecture wherever his power reached.

Antiochus IV Epiphanes, the Seleucid king whose persistent attempts to impose Greek culture and religion on the Jews resulted in the Maccabean rebellion.

The Ptolemies

When Alexander died at the age of 33, in 323 BCE, his four generals divided up his empire. Ptolemy took control of Egypt, while Seleucid ruled the eastern part of the old empire. Although these two rulers fought each other frequently they also encouraged the unity of the Greek, or Hellenistic, world. For a time Palestine – Israel and Judah – was ruled by the Ptolemies, but in 198 BCE it fell under Seleucid control. This saw the beginning of a time of persecution for the Jews. The ruler Antiochus IV Epiphanes profaned the Temple and decreed that Judaism was outlawed. A Jewish rebellion in 164 BCE led by Judas Maccabeus was successful and for almost a century the homeland of the Jews was relatively independent.

The Romans in Palestine

Gradually the Greek empire succumbed to the superior disciplined forces of the Romans, with Corinth falling in 146 BCE followed by Athens in 86 BCE. In 63 BCE the Roman general Pompey brought Syria and Palestine under Roman control before occupying

Although the Ptolemies were generally favourably disposed towards the Jews, the book of Maccabees (from the Apocrypha included in some Bibles) records a notable exception: Ptolemy IV tried to massacre the Jews by packing them into the hippodrome and setting drunken elephants on them.

Evidence of the Roman occupation abounds throughout Palestine. These are the remains of the Roman spa at Hammat Gader, south-east of the Sea of Galilee.

Greek culture soon followed Greek military conquests. Athletes depicted on a vase.

Jerusalem. Palestine's independence, always fragile, was finally ended. The Romans brought law, order and stability to the countries they conquered, as well as good roads, communications and many home comforts. In 31 BCE Octavian became the first ruler of the Roman empire and he adopted the title Caesar Augustus in 27 BCE. Jesus was born during his reign, in 5 or 4 BCE.

In many ways the time was opportune for the coming of Jesus. For a long while the people had been starved of any spiritual direction – the abstract philosophy of the Greeks and the materialism of the Romans failed to meet their basic spiritual needs. The only contemporary religion to offer any real spiritual guidance was Judaism and many Gentiles (non-Jews) found themselves irresistibly drawn towards it. The early Christians found that, with the general improvement in transport and communications, Jesus' message was able to move speedily through the Roman empire.

Jesus

Jesus is central to both the Christian faith and the Bible story. For millions of people he also stands at the crossroads of history – the transition between old and new, the bridge between God and humanity.

Jesus of Nazareth was called the 'Christ' (from the Hebrew word 'Messiah', meaning 'anointed one') because of his resurrection from the dead. From an early time this title became part of his name. Matthew and Luke tell us in their Gospels that Jesus was born in Bethlehem, Judea, towards the end of Herod the Great's reign (4 BCE), and was brought up in Nazareth, Galilee.

Baptism and temptation

Jesus was baptized in the River Jordan by John the Baptist in about 27 CE. This baptism was offered to everyone who wished to enter God's kingdom and so escape the coming divine judgment. Although Jesus' motives for requesting baptism are far from clear, the event marked the beginning of his public ministry. A time of temptation in the desert then followed before Jesus left home to begin preaching and teaching.

The ministry of Jesus

Jesus' ministry lasted no more

Christ's ministry involved the healing of those suffering mentally, physically and spiritually. *Christ Healing the Sick* by Rembrandt van Rijn (1606–69).

than three years and took place primarily in Galilee. One of the first things he did was to gather around himself a group of close friends, disciples or apostles, to share his life and continue his work after he was gone.

The kingdom of God was open to everyone but was welcomed, in particular, by the poor, the needy and the socially excluded. As the Gospels make clear, Jesus aimed his ministry mainly at the 'lost sheep of Israel', the Jews, although he responded to the needs of Gentiles who sought his help. He healed many who were sick in mind, body and spirit and he exorcized demons. He taught the people with compelling authority, although he was not formally trained as a rabbi. The ordinary people, though, regarded him as one.

The teaching of Jesus

In his teaching, conducted mainly through parables and short, pithy sayings, Jesus tried to encourage people to return to the true meaning of the Law by reducing the burden that the religious leaders placed on ordinary people. He preached about divine compassion and forgiveness, the acceptance of which brought salvation and the rejection of which spelled spiritual disaster. Above all else, he called men and women to a radical discipleship by showing them that would-be followers were called to give up their previous allegiances and follow him – even to death.

This was a controversial message and Jesus made many enemies by preaching it, particularly from among the Pharisees and Sadducees, the religious leaders of the time. They conspired together to have Jesus arrested and brought before the Sanhedrin, the Jewish council, and then Pontius Pilate, the Roman governor of Judea. It was Pilate who condemned Jesus to death and ordered his execution by crucifixion. Three days after Jesus died, in 30 CE, he was brought back to life by God. Belief in the resurrection of Jesus became the cornerstone of the early Church's preaching.

The Flagellation of Christ from a Romanesque Life of Christ and psalter. English, perhaps from Durham, 12th century.

Over the centuries, Jesus has been given many titles to summarize some aspect of his work on earth. These include Christ, Messiah, Lord, Saviour, Pioneer of Faith, Reconciler, Lamb of God, Victim, Sacrifice, Protector from God's Wrath, Mediator, Teacher, Healer, Peacemaker, Lord of the Cosmos and Liberator.

The Birth of Christianity

The Christian Church was born within weeks of Jesus' death, resurrection and ascension into heaven. Soon, being a Christian and belonging to a Christian community, the Church, became two sides of the same coin.

The ministry of Jesus ended with his ascension into heaven and the beginning of the 'era of the Holy Spirit'. At the beginning of this new era the Christian Church was established and began to spread its influence to the furthest reaches of the Roman empire.

The Day of Pentecost

The events that took place in Jerusalem on the Day of Pentecost, described in the Acts of the Apostles, mark the beginning of the Christian community and the start of its evangelistic mission to tell the world about Jesus Christ. This mission remains the prime responsibility of the Church today.

We are told that the disciples were gathered together in Jerusalem when the Holy Spirit came to rest on them, like tongues of fire, filling their mouths with many different languages. This dramatic image became a popular subject in later centuries for icons in the Eastern Orthodox Church and for sacred art in the West.

Belonging to the Christian community

The followers of Jesus came to be called 'Christians' at a very early stage, in Antioch. This underlines the distinctive

Antioch in Syria. Soon after the dispersion of believers from Jerusalem, Antioch became a thriving centre of Christianity, and it was the church here that sent out Paul on his first missionary journey.

> *Before Christ sent the Church into the world he sent the Spirit into the Church. The same order must be observed today.*
>
> JOHN STOTT, BRITISH THEOLOGIAN

characteristic of all disciples: their religious identity derives from Jesus the Christ, a title first given to Jesus by the early Church. A person was judged to be a Christian and a genuine member of the Christian community if they accepted Jesus as the Christ, as well as their Master, Lord, Saviour and Judge.

Christianity, however, has always been more than simply a matter of personal commitment. From the start it incorporated the sense of belonging to a public community, fellowship or Church. This community was spoken of from the time of Paul onwards as 'the body of Christ'. Belief in the divinity of Christ, baptism, participation in the Eucharist and an acceptance of the authority of the scriptures were not absolutely essential for church membership but they were laid down by the Church in later centuries.

The Missionary Journeys of Paul

Although Peter was the earliest leader of the Christian Church, it was Paul who gave it its shape and impetus. A Jewish convert to the faith, he undertook three long and arduous journeys, during which many people became Christians and many churches were established.

Despite political and religious opposition, the infant Christian Church gained many believers. Paul carried the Church beyond its Jewish roots and preached the new faith to the Gentiles. Saul, as he was originally known, was a strict Pharisaic Jew, born in Tarsus but with Roman citizenship, who studied in Jerusalem to be a rabbi. He led the Jewish opposition to Christianity in the area, but in 33 CE, while on his way to oppose the faith in Damascus, he was dramatically converted.

Paul the missionary

After spending some time in obscurity Paul emerged to help Barnabas establish the Christian faith in Antioch. In 47 CE, after a meeting in Jerusalem with the disciples Peter and James, he began a lifetime of travel, covering some 16,200 kilometres to spread the gospel. According to the Acts of the Apostles he made three extended tours, visiting most of the key towns and cities in Greece and Asia Minor:

◆ Tour one (45 or 46 CE) took him from his base in Syria in Antioch to Cyprus,

before travelling to present-day Turkey. He visited Attalia, Perga, Pisidian Antioch, Iconium, Derbe and Lystra before returning home by the same route.

◆ Tour two (48–51 CE) took him to the churches he had founded on the first journey, as well as to northern Greece – Philippi, Thessalonica, Athens and Berea. He returned by ship from Corinth via Ephesus and Caesarea to Antioch.

◆ Tour three (beginning in 53 CE) saw Paul travelling overland through Galatia and Phrygia in Turkey. He stayed for two years in Ephesus before being caught up in a riot and then travelling on through Philippi and Corinth.

Paul's strategy for evangelism was fairly clear: he set out to establish churches in the main towns and cities that were accessible on the excellent Roman roads. From there, local converts could take the Christian message into the more remote villages; at least one of the churches that he wrote to, in Colosse, was founded in this way. By the time of his third missionary journey most of the areas he visited had flourishing congregations. It was after this journey that Paul was arrested

I have worked much harder, been in prison more frequently, been flogged more severely, and been exposed to death again and again. Five times I received from the Jews the 40 lashes minus one. Three times I was beaten with rods, once I was stoned, three times I was shipwrecked, I spent a night and a day in the open sea... I have been in danger from rivers, in danger from bandits, in danger from my own countrymen, in danger from Gentiles; in danger in the city, in danger in the country, in danger at sea; and in danger from false brothers.

2 CORINTHIANS 11:23–26

in Jerusalem, where he was in prison between 58 and 60 CE, before being taken to Rome under guard. For two years Paul was under house arrest in the capital, although he was clearly able to receive visitors and preach the gospel to them, and that is where the story in Acts ends. It is widely assumed that Paul was executed during the persecution instituted by Nero in about 64 CE.

Ephesus, in present-day Turkey, was visited by Paul on his second and third missionary journeys. It boasted many fine buildings, including the Temple of Artemis, at the time the largest building in the Greek world. This is the façade of the Library of Celsus.

The Young Churches

The apostles were very active in the early years of Christianity and none more so than Paul. He established many churches in Asia Minor and his letters to them showed that he maintained a continuing interest in their spiritual progress.

By the end of the first century CE the Christian faith had spread throughout most of the Roman empire. The early Christian believers travelled widely to tell others about their faith in Christ and establish new churches.

The work of the apostles

The apostles were crucial in this early phase of Christianity. Peter was active in Rome, while Thomas travelled to India, John to Asia, Mark to Alexandria and Paul to Asia Minor. Some of the apostles were financed by wealthy members of the Church while others, like Paul, worked as they travelled to support themselves.

Paul was the most effective of these early missionaries. Not only did he establish many churches in the places he visited, but he also wrote highly treasured letters (epistles) to them, many of which are preserved in the New Testament. Among others, Paul wrote to Christian communities in Rome, Corinth, Philippi, Thessalonica, Ephesus and Colosse. These letters also had a much wider readership, since at some point they were collected together and circulated among communities familiar with his work. These letters contain the most extensive guide that we have to the beliefs and practices of the early Church, many of which Paul himself was very influential in forming.

The Church in action

At first the infant Christian Church was viewed as a sect of Judaism – just like the Pharisees and the Sadducees – and yet it extended a welcome to Gentiles as well as Jews. In the latter part of the first century, the Church became an all-embracing community, whose core membership mostly comprised Gentiles.

The early Christian communities were united by

In New Testament times the Roman empire extended across the Western Mediterranean and well beyond. This area was the cradle of Christianity.

Rome

ITALY

SICILY

The church at Philippi was special to Paul, for it was the first church he founded in Europe, and cared for him during his later travels and sufferings. Paul wrote that just as Philippi was a Roman outpost, so its church was an outpost of God's heavenly kingdom.

their common allegiance to the Jewish scriptures, which they believed pointed towards Jesus as the long-awaited Messiah. Membership of these communities was open to anyone who accepted Jesus as their Saviour and Lord. The unity of each community was expressed through the regular sharing of bread and wine at the Lord's Supper as an act of remembrance of the last meal that Jesus took with his disciples shortly before his death. Each local church also practised the rite of baptism, recited together the Lord's Prayer as part of their worship and fasted regularly.

The land stretching from the River Tigris and the River Euphrates, down through Assyria, along the Mediterranean Sea and southwards through Syria and Canaan to the Nile Valley is known as the Fertile Crescent. It was also the cradle of civilization, for here is where the earliest-known settled communities first attempted to farm the land, in around 10000 BCE.

The Sumerians were a key early civilization in the area and developed at the head of the Persian Gulf around 3500 BCE. Cities such as Byblos, Tyre, Haran, Damascus and Mari were built to act as bridgeheads for trade and the early movement of military convoys and weapons. Strong powers such as Egypt, Assyria and Babylon tried to control the territory around Jerusalem because of its strategic position and this led to their involvement in the events mentioned in the Old Testament.

Throughout this ancient world stories circulated about the origin of the world, the creation of human life and a great flood suffered as a punishment for human sin. Two such stories were particularly important:

◆ The Epic of Gilgamesh is a Babylonian story that tells of a flood sent by the gods as punishment for the sins of humankind and how an ancestor of Gilgamesh escaped the divine wrath in a ship that came to rest on Mount Ararat.
◆ In the book of Genesis a similar story is told about the creative activity of God, who brings the universe and

Successive empires of the ancient Near East have influenced biblical history.

all forms of life into being out of formless chaos. The climax of this divine creation is when the first man and woman are made. Their idyllic lives are soon destroyed, however, by the entry of sin and disobedience into the world. Humanity's steep moral decline comes to an abrupt end when God decides to bring an overwhelming flood to destroy everyone, apart from one family whose holiness of life qualifies it to replenish the earth after the flood has subsided. God provides Noah with a sign – a rainbow in the sky – as confirmation of his promise that he will never send such a flood again, no matter how badly the human race behaves in future.

> *Then God said, 'Let us make man in our image, in our likeness, and let them rule over the fish of the sea and the birds of the air, over the livestock, over all the earth, and over all the creatures that move along the ground.'*
>
> GENESIS 1:26

THE WORLD OF THE BIBLE

Contents

The Land of Palestine

Israel was not a large or powerful country, but its geographical location on a narrow strip of land between sea and desert gave it considerable economic and strategic importance.

The land in which the Israelites originally settled in the 13th century BCE after leaving Egyptian slavery was known as Canaan, but it was to change its name and boundaries more than once in the centuries that followed. Beginning as a single country, Israel, it split into the kingdoms of Israel and Judah after the death of Solomon and, much later, the Romans divided it into several regions – including Judea and Galilee. The later name of Palestine was derived from the Philistines, who moved into the narrow coastal strip about the same time as the Israelites conquered the central highlands under the leadership of Joshua.

Two lakes and one river

There are two inland seas in Israel, the Sea of Galilee and the Dead Sea. The River Jordan connects them both, flowing through a deep valley which was often flooded. The river forms the backbone of the country. It rises in the Lebanon mountains and is fed by numerous small

The land occupied by the Israelites was traditionally described as running from 'Dan to Beersheba' and if you look at the map you can see why. This tiny area was less than 230 kilometres long and only 80 kilometres wide at its broadest point – the northern tip of the Dead Sea. The southern tip of the Dead Sea is 400 kilometres below sea level, the lowest inhabited point on the earth's surface.

In the south of Israel the fertile hill country gives way to the arid landscape of the Negev.

tributaries, such as the Cherith. The Sea of Galilee, also known in the Gospels as Gennesaret or Tiberias, is a freshwater lake about 21 kilometres long and 12.8 kilometres wide and has an abundant stock of fish. The Dead Sea is much larger but, as its name suggests, almost nothing survives in its extremely salty waters.

Physical geography

Two valleys cut across the centre of Israel from the Mediterranean Sea in the west to the River Jordan: the plain of Megiddo and the valley of Jezreel. The main range of mountains runs from north to south, just to the west of the Jordan, from Upper Galilee to the desert. West of the mountains, by the Mediterranean, and south of the plain of Megiddo, are the fertile plains of Philistia and Sharon.

To the north these plains are interrupted by the Carmel range of hills, in the middle of which is a pass at Megiddo. This was the vital point for controlling military and commercial traffic between Egypt, Syria and the east. It was also the scene of some important battles, including the unsuccessful attempt by King Josiah of Judah to halt the Egyptians.

Several mountains are mentioned in the Bible, including Hermon, a few kilometres from Dan, Tabor, west of the Sea of Galilee, and Sinai, south of Palestine and north of the Red Sea. The wilderness around Sinai was linked to Beersheba by a desert area known as the Negev.

The Regions of Palestine

The geography of the land of Palestine fell naturally into seven regions. Jesus spent most of his life in the southern part of Galilee before making his final journey to Jerusalem.

The landscape of Palestine was richly varied.

The coastal plain
When the Israelites first moved into Canaan they lived in the central highlands and made sporadic attempts to conquer the coastal area – only recently occupied by the Philistines who were firmly entrenched there in five city-states. Attempts to bring the whole country under Israelite control were largely fruitless because the Philistines had discovered how to smelt and use iron to make weapons and chariots, giving them an overwhelming military advantage. In any case the coastal area was only of limited value to the Israelites, since there were few natural harbours and they were an agricultural, not a seafaring, nation.

Galilee
North of Mount Carmel the land opened out into the broad and fertile plain of Esdraelon. Beyond this lay the trees and valleys surrounding the inland

Walled fields and olive groves typify the cultivated land of the central highlands.

Sea of Galilee. The southern part of Galilee was the location for many of the Gospel narratives, as it was there that Jesus lived and carried out most of his ministry.

The Jordan valley
The land rises gently from the Mediterranean to about 1,000 metres above sea level before dropping precipitously down the great gash in the earth's surface formed by the Jordan rift valley, a trench which can be traced all the way to East Africa. The River Jordan itself flows from Mount Hermon, through the Sea of Galilee to the Dead Sea. This valley was inhabited from about 5000 BCE and city-states began to emerge towards the end of the fourth millennium BCE.

The Golan Hills, east of the Sea of Galilee.

The central highlands
The hills of Samaria and the Judean hills to the south are part of the 'backbone' of rough, rocky uplands. When the Israelites first moved into the area its fortified towns proved relatively easy to defend. Although this area contained the capital city of Jerusalem there were few roads which passed through.

The town of Samaria was built in 880 BCE and besieged by the Assyrians in 721 BCE before 27,000 captives were deported and replaced by colonists from the Assyrian empire. Samaria was destroyed by Alexander in the fourth century BCE but rebuilt later by Pompey and Herod the Great.

The Transjordan
This is a fertile but mountainous area with good rainfall providing excellent pasture land for large flocks of sheep in biblical times.

The Shephelah
An area of low foothills between the coastal plain and the central highlands formed a buffer between the Philistines on the coast and the Israelites inland. There were constant skirmishes along the fortified roads and villages of the area.

The plain of Megiddo
A string of mountain ranges runs the whole length of Palestine some distance back from the coast. A break in this mountain range meant that the land dropped to a height of little more than 100 metres, dividing the central highlands from Galilee and the northern mountains. This was the location for the most important ancient trade-route linking Egypt to Damascus, in Syria, and Mesopotamia.

Climate

Palestine had remarkable variations in temperature, rainfall and vegetation for a land of its size. Its inhabitants learned to use these variations to make it both productive and fertile.

Palestine's climate was hot in the summer, with little rain, and cool in the winter. The 'former and latter rains' mentioned by the prophet Jeremiah fell at the beginning and end of the winter and were essential for a good harvest.

Temperature

On the shores of the Dead Sea temperatures could exceed 40 degrees Celsius, while just 160 kilometres away, in Upper Galilee, snow could be falling. Elsewhere, even in winter, a balmy day could be followed by a freezing night, giving a very wide daily fluctuation in temperature.

Rainfall

The level of rainfall in the different regions of Palestine depended to a large extent on the height above sea level. Generally, the further south the lower the rainfall. The rain fell mainly in the winter season, which began in the middle of September, with the heaviest rain falling in December and January. There was slightly less rain until late March or early April when the drier weather arrived. The summers were very dry, with little or no rainfall likely between the middle of June and September. Families and flocks often migrated to seek

The Dead Sea was 74 kilometres long and up to 16 kilometres wide. Water evaporated from the surface of the water at the rate of 1,500 millimetres a year because of the heat.

The land rises gradually across Israel from Gaza on the coast to Jerusalem in the Judean hills. The land then drops abruptly at the Jordan valley, where Jericho is situated. The average temperature decreases gradually from west to east, but then soars around Jericho. Annual rainfall increases from west to east, but decreases dramatically in the Jordan valley.

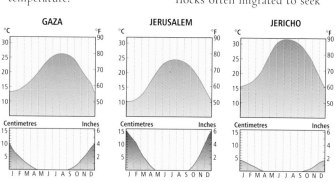

snows of Mount Hermon, it emptied into the Dead Sea from which water evaporated rapidly.

As the cities in Palestine grew in size so the problem of keeping them permanently supplied with water became acute. Towns, cities and villages were generally dependent on local wells and springs for their water supply, but the city of Jerusalem installed elaborate waterworks to meet the needs of its growing population. The right of access to such supplies was a very highly sought privilege and ferociously guarded. If the supply of water to any place was blocked, deliberately or accidentally, then death was not far behind.

The wide variety of vegetation found in Palestine reflected its range of temperature and rainfall. Desert scrub and steppeland in the south gave way to the forests and lush pasture land of Lebanon in the north.

The Dead Sea is fed by the River Jordan, but has no outlet. High temperatures cause rapid evaporation and 25 per cent of the water consists of concentrated chemical deposits.

more fertile lands during the frequent droughts.

Water

The conservation of water was a very important part of everyday life in Palestine. The only river of any size was the Jordan and, although this was fed throughout the year by the

Trees and Plants

There were not many different tree species in Palestine during biblical times, but there was a wide variety of herbs and plants.

Although Palestine was never densely forested, the tree cover in biblical times was much greater than it is today. The wide climatic variations encouraged an unusually large range of plants and herbs, although many of those mentioned in the Bible are now difficult to identify with certainty.

Trees

The acacia tree, the 'tree of the desert', was used by the Israelites to build the Ark of the Covenant as well as parts of the Tabernacle, the tent in which the Ark was kept. Oaks, firs, cypresses and pines flourished in the hilly parts of the country, while water-loving trees such as poplars, willows and oleanders grew in thickets along the banks of the Jordan.

Fruiting trees were commercially important to the area. The almond tree was valued for its oil and nuts and admired for the beauty of its blossom, which was depicted in the carvings on the Ark of the Covenant. The date palm flourished in the Jordan valley;

A lone acacia tree near the Dead Sea. One of the few trees of any size to be found growing in the Sinai desert, acacias provided the wood used in the construction of the Ark of the Covenant.

Wild flowers still grow in profusion on the hills of Galilee.

Jericho was known as 'the city of palm trees'. This tall and slender tree became a national symbol in Palestine for victory and rejoicing as well as being used in the Old Testament to symbolize grace and uprightness. Although few cedars now remain in Lebanon the tree was exported in vast quantities in Old Testament times. It was a very durable wood that could be easily carved and was used extensively to panel Solomon's Temple and palace.

Plants and herbs

The hillsides of Galilee in the spring were a riot of flowers and Jesus referred to them collectively as 'lilies of the valley'. These would have included crocuses, poppies anemones, crown marguerites, narcissi and cyclamens. Myrtle was a common shrub on Palestinian hillsides, with its fragrant leaves and flowers. In the Old Testament Isaiah used this plant to symbolize God's great generosity.

Many species of wormwood grew in Palestine, all of which tasted bitter. Not surprisingly, the word was used metaphorically in the Bible to suggest unhappiness, sorrow and disaster. The mandrake was a flowering herb of the nightshade family which was known for its aphrodisiac qualities and its ability to assist with conception – something of which Rachel and Leah, Jacob's wives, were obviously aware in their story in Genesis. Herbs and spices were highly valued as medicinal aids and flavouring for food. Among the common herbs found in Palestine were garlic, anise, hyssop, cumin, dill, mint and mustard. Jesus referred to the tiny mustard seed in one of his parables as a suitable picture for the growth of the kingdom of God from very small beginnings.

On more than one occasion Jesus referred to the 'thorns' which grew everywhere in Palestine stifling the growing seed after it was planted. Unfortunately we cannot know just which thorns Jesus was referring to as there are more than 120 species of them in Israel!

45

Marriage and Family Life

Mothers and fathers had clearly defined roles within Jewish families. The father took total responsibility for his family's material well-being, while the mother organized all aspects of household management.

The modern ideal of a man and a woman living together in lifelong monogamy was foreign to the early Old Testament world. The founder of the Jewish nation, Abraham, had two wives, but by the time the monarchy was founded in Israel polygamy appears to have been restricted to the royal household.

Each ordinary family unit was basically self-sustaining. Food was stored in the house and animals were also kept there. The family was patriarchal: the father had absolute authority

A wife of noble character
who can find?
She is worth far more than rubies...
She selects wool and flax and
works with eager hands...
She gets up while it is still dark;
she provides food for her family...
She sets about her work vigorously;
her arms are strong for her tasks...
She speaks with wisdom.

PROVERBS 31:10, 13, 15, 17, 26

A Jewish marriage contract, Italy, 16th century.

over his own relations except in those areas, such as household management, where he chose to delegate it. The writer of the book of Proverbs spelled out the responsibilities expected of the dutiful Jewish wife and they were very heavy. Children

FAMILY RELATIONSHIPS

The basis for a loving family atmosphere was believed to be a due reverence for God and his teachings in the Torah. The father of the family was considered to be God's representative and was expected to exercise a stern discipline over his children based on the teachings of the scriptures. This discipline was supposed to be firm and fair without, at any time, provoking his children to rebel. In extreme cases, though, the Torah did allow parents to have perpetually disobedient children put to death!

remained in their father's control at least until marriage and, on his death, this control passed to his eldest son. Any family inheritance was passed down the male line, with the eldest son taking a double share. It only passed to the females in the family if they had no male siblings.

Marriage

In the early Old Testament period polygamy was the norm and it made sense for each family to have as many children as possible, since they looked after their parents in old age. The choice of a marriage partner was arranged within the same clan or extended family, with first cousins as the preferred option. By the time of the New Testament marriage fell into two parts:

◆ the betrothal: the signing of a marriage contract in front of two witnesses — a contract which could only be dissolved by divorce.

◆ the completion of the marriage process when the groom 'collected' his bride and took her home with him to his house.

Two financial transactions took place as part of a largely civil wedding ceremony. The groom or his family paid a sum of money to the bride's father, who held it in case he or his daughter's husband died. The bride's father gave a dowry to his daughter or her new husband, which could take the form of money, property, land or servants.

Education

It was not until the New Testament period that education outside the home began to develop in Palestine. Boys attended the local synagogue to be educated by the rabbi in the Jewish religious traditions, but the education of girls continued at home.

We know very little about education in early Israel except that the moral and religious education of children was seen as the prime responsibility of parents, especially the mother. The father was largely involved in the transmission of his practical skills to the boys in the family, whether for farming or fighting!

A calendar found at Gezer which lists the agricultural tasks for the year. It is written in the form of a schoolchild's rhyme.

The family was at the centre of the transmission of faith and ritual from one generation to another – the most important aspect of education. The ritual at the heart of the Passover festival, for instance, was kept alive largely within the family; this festival remains essentially a family celebration today.

In the New Testament period it seems likely that the majority of converts to Christianity were illiterate, but there were opportunities for them to learn to read and write. Before long, Christians were to be found in the literary and philosophical schools of the time.

THE ORAL TRADITION

Among rabbis and their pupils emphasis was placed upon learning things by heart; in this way the oral tradition was faithfully transmitted and extended. As a result of this kind of education the ability to retain information for a long time became a well-developed skill. This was crucial in the years following Jesus' ministry, when most of the information about Jesus was retained and circulated by word of mouth. Although there is little evidence to suggest that Jesus actually based his teaching on the method of the rabbis, many of his sayings were cast in such a way as to make them stick in the memory. After Jesus was gone, such sayings were retained and given a prominent position in the Gospel narratives.

> *Heaven and earth will pass away,*
> *but my words will never pass away.*
>
> MATTHEW 24:35

In New Testament times

By the time of Jesus early education for boys and girls remained a family responsibility, but from an early age boys were sent to be educated by the local rabbi in the synagogue. According to the Talmud there were 480 synagogues with schools attached in Jerusalem alone. The rabbi did not usually charge a fee, preferring instead to earn his living by plying some trade or craft, very much as Paul did when he worked to finance his teaching and preaching ministry.

A Greek schoolboy's workbook with seven wooden 'pages'. Such pages were usually coated on one side with wax, so that writing could be scratched into them using a stylus. However, this example was not coated, suggesting that it contained notes that the owner needed to keep for some time.

Food and Drink

Food and drink were integral to social and religious life. Eating and fasting have always been significant features of the Jewish faith, while the Christian ceremony of Communion was based on a common fellowship meal.

Nearly all of the farming and food production in Israel was on a subsistence basis, with people growing enough to meet the needs of their own family. Unreliable rainfall and frequent droughts often upset this arrangement; locusts and other pests were also an ever-present threat to food supplies – as were invading and marauding armies.

Oats and barley still grow wild in Palestine. In Bible times, barley formed the major part of the diet of the poor.

Cereal and dairy foods

Cereal crops provided the staple diet of people in Israel, who valued wheat more highly than barley (barley flour was only used by the poorer members of society). Both wheat and barley were used to make flat cake bread. Milk was used from the earliest times, when semi-nomadic tribes largely lived off the dairy products of their flocks. Although these products were in everyday use they were still greatly appreciated, as the description of the Jewish Promised Land of Canaan as a 'land flowing with milk and honey' testifies. Honey was a much-prized delicacy and was the only form of sweetening available for use in cakes.

Vegetables and fruit

When the Israelites spent 40 years in the wilderness travelling to Canaan they remembered, with deep nostalgia, the cucumbers, leeks, onions and garlic that they had eaten in Egypt. The range of

Excavations at Gibeon show that the wealthy valued wine highly. A wine cellar excavated there had the capacity to hold 100,000 litres of wine at a steady temperature of 18 degrees Celsius.

A basalt olive press at Capernaum. Olives were placed in the depression in the lower stone. The top stone was rotated by means of a shaft fixed through its hole.

DIETARY LAWS

Strict dietary laws in the Torah prohibited the eating of pork, rabbit, camel, any animal killed violently and any meat containing blood. Part of the process of making an animal fit to eat involved the draining out of all blood. There was also a prohibition on cooking or eating meat and milk products which were prepared together. During the Passover festival special laws were in place which permitted only the eating of unleavened bread, with no leavened food allowed in the house.

vegetables grown in Israel was more limited, although lentils and beans were popular. As for fruit, olives provided oil and grapes were either eaten fresh or dried as raisins. Grapes were also made into wine, which was the basic drink. Figs were popular both as food and also for medicinal purposes. The nuts available included almonds and pistachios.

Meat and fish

Meat was not a staple part of the diet in Israel and was only eaten on special occasions or when guests were in the home, hence the 'fatted calf' served up for Abraham's angelic visitors and for the prodigal son in one of Jesus' parables. Fish was much more part of the everyday diet, and there are many references in the Gospels indicating this, including the account in Luke's Gospel of the resurrected Jesus eating a fish breakfast with his disciples.

Spices on sale at a market in Beer Sheva. Spice caravans pioneered the trade routes from Asia through Mesopotamia to Egypt.

Working Life

The main occupation in first-century Palestine was farming, although a thriving fishing industry was centred around the Sea of Galilee. A few Palestinians worked for the occupying forces, but they were among the most despised people in society.

Most families in Palestine were just self-sufficient, owning and farming a small plot of land. While the men farmed or followed a trade the women ran the household, often spinning or weaving to make extra money. Parents passed on their skills to their children, who were expected to play a full part in the family business from an early age.

The livestock kept included sheep, goats, oxen and asses, but Jewish farmers were forbidden from keeping pigs. Asses were used for carrying heavy loads, while oxen were used for pulling the plough. On special occasions an ox might be killed for its meat, as would a sheep, although sheep were mainly kept for their wool.

Farming

Farming was hard manual work, involving ploughing, sowing, reaping, cultivating grapes and olives and tending sheep. The land was ploughed in the rainy season before the farmer walked his fields scattering the seed. The story about the sower told by Jesus in Mark's Gospel graphically illustrates the wastefulness of this method of sowing. Olives were harvested between September and November, flax in March or April, and wheat from May to June. Fruit was harvested in August or September.

The farming year in Israel.

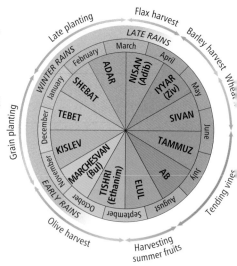

THE WORLD OF THE BIBLE

The work of a shepherd was no rural idyll. Shepherds spent all their lives in the open, facing possible dangers and enduring considerable extremes of temperature.

Shepherding

Being a shepherd and living with the sheep was a full-time occupation in first-century Palestine. Each night the animals were kept in rough stone enclosures and the shepherd slept across the entrance. There was a constant danger from wild animals and thieves. If sheep or goats were stolen the shepherd had to recompense their owner, while for those killed by wild animals physical evidence of the attack had to be provided.

Fishing

Fishermen often worked together because the work was heavy and onerous, involving salting, drying, selling, mending the nets and repairing the boats to keep them in working order. Although some fishermen earned their living by throwing a net from the shore, serious fishermen

worked in pairs from boats to cast a dragnet, with its weights and floats, into the water. The heaviest work involved dragging the net back on board when it was full of fish.

The demands of working life in Palestine were made even greater by the different taxes to which the ordinary male citizen was liable. (Females were not liable to pay these taxes.) He made an annual payment of a half-shekel for the upkeep of the Temple, which was collected by officials travelling the country. There was also a payment to the Herodian rulers and taxes to Rome. Little wonder, then, that there was widespread resentment among the working population. Most people had to work all their lives until they were physically incapable.

Village and Town Life

Life in Israel was largely agrarian and based originally upon the village. Later, it became necessary for people to move into towns for their own protection. By the time of Jesus these towns had become very sophisticated communities under Greek and Roman influence.

In biblical times villages were unwalled settlements which left people without means of defending themselves, while towns were surrounded by a wall and built close to a water supply. The earliest settlements in Israel were villages; archaeological excavations show that people were farming in or around the city of Jericho by 6000 BCE.

Village life

The first villages were probably little more than the huddled tents of nomads, who moved on and settled elsewhere as the seasons changed. Village life came to centre on farming; oil obtained from olives was used for medicine, cooking and lighting. Out of necessity villages grew up as close to available water supplies as possible.

Town life

The first towns became established around 4000 BCE because of the growing need of people to be able to defend themselves effectively. For a time many people continued to live in villages but went to the nearest town when they felt threatened or the weather deteriorated. Entry into a town

The city gate into Jerusalem. The gate of a city was not only an important part of its defences, but was also where the elders gathered for discussion, and where business was transacted.

was through a single gateway which was narrow and heavily defended. Most people arrived each morning to carry out their business and tended to stay close to the gate once inside. This area was the beating heart of the town: legal transactions, disputes and commercial activity were all conducted there. It was at such a place that Boaz acquired Ruth as his wife and where he took possession of her family property from her closest male relative.

Herod the Great constructed the coastal town of Caesarea in honour of Caesar Augustus. The higher of two aqueducts carried water nine kilometres from the southern slopes of Mount Carmel.

The influence of the Greeks and the Romans meant that towns built in the New Testament period were more carefully planned. Buildings, often several stories high, were set in narrow streets and emphasis was on the town as a place of commerce rather than refuge. The Romans built aqueducts to bring water into towns and cities, as well as public baths and efficient drainage systems. When King Herod the Great built Samaria and Caesarea he used a Roman plan with the main street running through the centre of the city, crossed by lesser roads at right-angles, and houses built in blocks of four.

LANDOWNING

When the Israelites first entered Canaan the 12 tribes were each given plots of land. The land was then divided equally between the people in each tribe, but this equality was eroded when the monarchy was established and large estates began to swallow up smaller parcels of land. A wealthy and increasingly influential class of bureaucrats sprang up and took every opportunity to oppress the poor. The poor became very poor, so that labourers were forced to hire themselves out for a pittance. It was this practice that brought the most vehement criticism from the prophets.

Travel and Transport

Travelling was a necessary and often uncomfortable fact of life in biblical times. Travel was mainly on foot, but camels and asses were also used; some nations also built ships. By Roman times an extensive road network made travelling much easier.

Despite all its problems and dangers, travelling was common in biblical times: Abraham's journey into Canaan, Jacob travelling down into Egypt, the Israelites journeying through the desert and Paul's journeys to preach the gospel are just a few of the epic journeys mentioned in the Bible.

Travel in the Old Testament
In Old Testament times there were very few paved roads in Palestine and, while the great seafaring nations of Egypt and Phoenicia were building warships and sailing vessels, the Israelites were essentially a land-based nation with a deep-seated fear of the sea. The only exception to this appears to have been during the reign of Solomon, when a fleet of ships was built for trading purposes; even then, outside help was needed from Hiram, king of Tyre, because the necessary expertise was not available in Israel.

Egypt developed the chariot for military and civilian use by about 2600 BCE. Chariot wheels were made by slicing timber in the direction of the grain into two semicircles and then joining them together using two strips of wood.

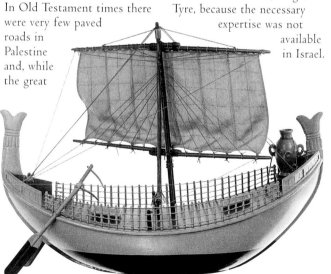

A model of a ship similar to that used by Solomon's merchant navy.

The uplands of Judea are not well served by roads, even today. It is not difficult to imagine the story of the Good Samaritan being enacted on a road like this one close to Jericho.

Travel in the New Testament

The efficient and extensive system of roads established by the Romans made travel in and around Israel much easier – so much so that carriages could be used by the wealthy. However, such roads only went in the directions that the Romans considered necessary for their own purpose, which was to move goods and troops around their empire. Elsewhere, roads were either non-existent or inadequate, wide enough for little more than a man leading his donkey. Jesus' parable of the good Samaritan provides a glimpse of the problems associated with such roads.

The ass was domesticated in Palestine long before either the horse or the camel and was the main beast of burden as well as the most popular means of general transport. Although horses were usually reserved for use in war during the Old Testament period, they were used more widely by civilians in the time of the New Testament, although they could not carry much and were expensive to keep.

Throughout Bible times traders often covered long journeys in convoy – forming a caravan – both for company and also as a way of protecting themselves against raiders and bandits. There were recognized caravan routes and these crossed Palestine in all directions. These routes were commercially of great importance to the land of Palestine, which was thin and largely bounded by the Mediterranean Sea to the west and the Syrian desert to the east. All traffic moving between Mesopotamia and Arabia, Egypt and the rest of Africa had to pass through a narrow corridor no more than 120 kilometres wide. Important cities grew up along this route and tolls were exacted from caravan trains passing through.

A Roman milestone near Capernaum.

Feasts and Holy Days

The Jews celebrated the weekly festival of the Sabbath as a time of remembrance and rest. They also celebrated several annual festivals, most notably the Passover, to express thankfulness for all God had done for them, and for regular events in the agricultural year.

From their earliest times the Israelites kept fasts and festivals as a part of their religion and way of life. The festivals gradually became a mix of agricultural celebrations and times to remember God's dealings with the nation of Israel. Later, the historical aspect of the festival took precedence.

The Sabbath

The Sabbath day was Israel's most distinctive festival and, unlike the other festivals, it was celebrated weekly, not annually. The seventh day of each week was set aside, as God commanded in the scriptures, to be a day of total rest for animals and humans alike. It was a day when Jews were commanded to

The seventh month in the Jewish calendar, the month of Tishri, was the most solemn of the year. On the first day of this month trumpets were sounded for a special celebration that introduced a day of rest and relaxation even more important than the Sabbath itself.

Orthodox Jews venerate copies of the Torah during a festival at the Western Wall in Jerusalem.

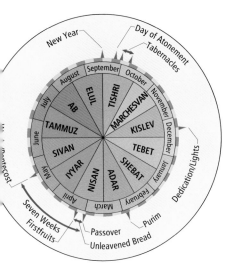

The Passover

The Passover (also known as the Festival of Unleavened Bread or Pesach) was the most important annual Jewish festival. It took place on the evening of the 14th of Nisan, when each family sacrificed a lamb as a reminder of the time when the 'Angel of Death' passed over each Israelite house before killing every Egyptian first-born – the last of the 10 plagues. By the time of Jesus the Passover was the main 'pilgrimage festival' which drew Jews from all over the Roman empire to worship in the Temple in Jerusalem.

Pentecost and Tabernacles

The two other pilgrimage festivals were Pentecost, or Shavuot, a time of great rejoicing which took place 50 days after Passover and marked the end of the harvest, and the Festival of Tabernacles, or *Sukkot*, which took place in autumn to mark the fruit-crop harvest. The celebrations for this festival included building tabernacles as a reminder of the time when the Israelites spent 40 years travelling in the wilderness towards their Promised Land. Jews still celebrate these festivals today.

The religious festivals of the Jewish year.

remember all that God had done for them, especially in rescuing their ancestors from Egyptian slavery. The day was also a recognition that rest and leisure, as much as work, were part of God's intended pattern for life.

OTHER HOLY DAYS

By the time of Jesus there were other feasts or holy days which were celebrated in the Jewish community. At the end of the summer the people were called to a fast before the New Year, or Rosh Hashanah, began, ending with the Day of Atonement, or Yom Kippur, when the people sought God's forgiveness for their past sins through repentance. This was the only day on which the High Priest could enter the Holy of Holies, which was the innermost part of the Temple complex in Jerusalem.

The Temple

The existence of the Temple in Israel's capital city of Jerusalem signified the presence of God among his people. Three buildings were successively erected on the same site before the Romans finally destroyed the Temple for ever in 70 CE.

The three Temples were constructed between the times of Solomon in the 10th century BCE and Herod the Great in the first century BCE. Each of them was dedicated to the worship of God.

The first Temple

Plans to build a central shrine for national worship in Jerusalem were first mooted by David and carried out by his son, Solomon, in the 10th century BCE. Solomon built his Temple on the eastern hill of the city where the Dome of the Rock, a very important Muslim shrine, is located today. Solomon's building was rectangular with a porch facing east, a nave and an inner sanctuary, the Holy of Holies. The entire structure was lined with gold and the innermost shrine was inlaid with pure gold. The holiest place contained the Ark of the Covenant and the entire building was surrounded by two courtyards. Having been plundered several times this first Temple was finally destroyed by King Nebuchadnezzar of Babylon in 587/6 BCE.

The second Temple

The prophet Ezekiel had a vision of a new Temple in 571 BCE, but it was never built. Those exiles who later drifted back to Israel from Babylon did build another Temple on the same site, but it was much smaller than Solomon's. The work was completed in 515 BCE. Although the building stood for more than 500 years little is known about it, except that it was defiled by the Seleucid ruler Antiochus IV Epiphanes, who ruled from 175 to 164 BCE. This led to a revolt of the Jews under their leader Judas Maccabeus. The Temple was subsequently rededicated, an event which is celebrated annually by Jews at the Festival of Dedication, or Hanukkah.

The third Temple

Herod the Great did not tear down the second Temple when

According to Josephus, the Jewish historian, the Romans began to destroy the Temple on the 10th day of the fifth month in 70 CE. This was the same day of the year when the first Temple had been burned to the ground by the king of Babylon.

An artist's impression of Solomon's Temple. The main room was the Holy Place, and contained the incense altar, the table of showbread and five pairs of candlesticks. The Holy of Holies was the smaller room furthest from the doors, and was entered by a priest just once a year. It housed the Ark of the Covenant, which was overshadowed on either side by winged creatures. All interior walls were lined with pine covered with gold.

he decided to refurbish and rebuild it; with his unpopularity among the Jews that would surely have led to a riot. Instead, he made certain that worship could continue uninterrupted and the main work took just 18 months. Built on the same plan as Solomon's Temple, Herod's construction was by far the grandest, with the whole building covered in solid gold. A covered cloister ran right around the outer courtyards. The main entrance, from the south, led into the first of the courtyards, called the Court of the

Gentiles. This space was open to all, but notices in Latin and Greek forbade any non-Jew from going further on pain of death. The next courtyard was the Court of Women, which was as far as women could go unless they were presenting an offering. Jewish men could enter the Court of Israel and even take part in a procession in the Court of Priests during the Festival of Tabernacles.

New Testament Religion

As long as the Temple stood in Jerusalem it was the national centre of Jewish religious life although, in practice, this had come to depend far more on the local synagogue by the time of Jesus.

In New Testament times prayer, studying the Torah, attending services in the synagogue, regular fasting, keeping the Sabbath day and celebrating the religious festivals were the basic components of Jewish spiritual life.

Israel's faith

From its inception Judaism was always a fiercely monotheistic faith committed to the belief that, in the beginning, God had created everything and called the early patriarchs and ancestors into a special relationship with him, a covenant, which was based on mutual trust and faith. The main features of this covenant were laid out in the Torah, the Law which all Jews were expected to keep as a sign of their good faith and commitment to God. The

The early fifth-century synagogue in the Galilean town of Capernaum possibly stands on the site of the one in which Jesus preached. The classical style of its architecture resembles that of the synagogue at Korazin three kilometres away.

> *Hear, O Israel: the Lord our God,*
> *the Lord is one. Love the Lord your*
> *God with all your heart and with all*
> *your soul and with all your strength.*
>
> THE *SHEMA*, DEUTERONOMY 6:4–7

Shema, repeated daily, was as close as Judaism came to having a statement of faith, with its insistence that God is the only God, and that all other gods and deities are empty idols.

The Temple and the synagogue

Keeping the Torah and its many laws was fundamental to all Jews. Jews were taught that a perfect obedience to the Torah might hasten the coming of the long-expected and longed-for Messiah, who would deliver the people from all their enemies and establish God's kingdom on earth. Although by the time of Jesus Jewish men and women were much more likely to be found worshipping in their local synagogue than the Temple, it was not until after the Temple was destroyed in 70 CE that the synagogue assumed the central place in Jewish worship for everyone.

> *The ancestral*
> *custom is to obey*
> *the priest of the*
> *God whom we*
> *worship.*
>
> FLAVIUS JOSEPHUS
> (37–c. 95 CE),
> JEWISH HISTORIAN

After this happened it was the rabbi and not the Temple priest who became the main inspiration in Jewish society for understanding and interpreting the Torah. Sacrifices ceased with the events of 70 CE and synagogue services became very important. The synagogue served as the local school and the centre for local government, as well as the place for holding political meetings, charitable associations and a law court.

During the time of Jesus, however, many people outside Jerusalem made every effort to reach the Temple in Jerusalem for the three great pilgrimage festivals of Passover, Pentecost and Tabernacles. The Temple was also where outstanding rabbis taught, under the colonnades of the Court of the Gentiles. After his dramatic entrance into Jerusalem riding on a donkey at the beginning of the last week in his life, Jesus spent some time teaching and disputing in this very place.

The word 'Bible' comes from the Greek word *biblia*, meaning 'books', and its plural form draws our attention to the fact that the Bible, both Jewish and Christian, is not a single volume but a collection – a library – of books. The Old Testament, the Jewish scriptures, reached something like its present form around 1000 BCE, while the latest books in the New Testament were accepted as authoritative by about 100 CE. Official religious recognition, however, did not come until much later.

The books in the Old and New Testaments combined (the Christian Bible) are very diverse. Most of them passed through a lengthy process of editing, interpretation, reinterpretation, adaptation and expansion in the course of their long transmission. Biblical criticism can help us unravel some of this process, although the findings of biblical scholars can only remain, at best, tentative.

The Old Testament consists of 24 books split into three groupings: the Law (the Torah), the Prophets and the Writings. Some of the historical books are split in two, giving 39 books in total. These books comprise:

◆ the Torah, of which there are five books (Genesis, Exodus, Leviticus, Numbers and Deuteronomy)

Torah on display at the Western Wall, Jerusalem.

◆ the prophets, of which there are
21 books, including Joshua, 1 and
2 Kings, Isaiah and Malachi
◆ the Writings, of which there are
13 books, including Ruth, 1 and
2 Chronicles and Psalms.

The New Testament includes a further
27 books which can be divided into:

◆ historical books, which are the four
Gospels and the Acts of the Apostles
◆ epistles, which are letters written
by Paul, Peter, John and others
◆ apocalyptic literature, which is
the book of Revelation.

> *Had the Bible been in clear
> straightforward language, had the
> ambiguities and contradictions been edited
> out and had the language been constantly
> modernized to accord with contemporary
> taste it would almost certainly have
> been... a work of lesser importance.*
>
> J.K. GALBRAITH, HISTORIAN AND ECONOMIST

THE MAKING OF THE BIBLE

Contents

The Text of the Bible

The Bible is a collection of books which were written at different times and by many different authors. None of the original manuscripts has survived.

Scholars have tried to find the earliest and most reliable text of the Bible. Clearly it is vital that Christians should be able to read for themselves what the authors of the different books really said, or as close to it as possible.

The Old Testament text
The earliest translation of the Jewish scriptures was the Septuagint (also known as the LXX), which was a translation from Hebrew to Greek to meet the needs of Jews who had been dispersed throughout the Greek-speaking world and did

> *Significant progress has been made in the study of the biblical text over the past two centuries. Instead of poorly edited Hebrew and Greek texts scholars and students can now have ready access to carefully edited versions which are filled with textual information.*
>
> BART D. EHRMAN,
> 20TH-CENTURY BIBLICAL SCHOLAR

St Jerome Reading in a Landscape by Giovanni Bellini (c. 1430–1516).

not speak Hebrew. It provided the basis for many subsequent translations, most notably the very influential Latin Vulgate version of St Jerome in 382 CE.

Translations of the Jewish scriptures using the Hebrew text were generally taken from the Masoretic version. The Masoretes were a group of Jewish scholars working between 500 and 1000 BCE, who added vowels to the Hebrew text which, until this time, had consisted purely of consonants. To preserve the sanctity of the ancient text Masorete scholars added marks above and below the lines of writing so as not to disturb the text itself.

The reliability of the Masoretes' work can be tested by comparing it to some of the Dead Sea Scrolls – maunscripts which are around 1,000 years older than any other Hebrew version of the scriptures and so probably more accurate. Such a comparison only serves to enhance our respect for the reliability of the other, much older, Hebrew texts that we have.

The New Testament text

There are thousands of Greek manuscripts of the New Testament in existence. The oldest virtually complete manuscripts date from the fourth and fifth centuries CE. There are also papyrus fragments dating from the second and third centuries CE. Other manuscripts are on parchment and all were bound in the form of books (codices). These provide a continuous text, either in the form of 'uncials' (upper-case letters) or 'minuscules' (lower-case letters). In these codices there are no spaces between the words, no punctuation marks and no division into chapters and verses. The most important uncials are the *Codex Sinaiticus* and the *Codex Vaticanus* of the fourth century CE. The *Codex Bezae* contains both the Greek and Latin text of the Gospels and the Acts of the Apostles. The earliest fragment of a papyrus manuscript is of a short extract from John 18 which was discovered in Egypt and published in 1935; this fragment has been dated at about 135 CE.

The Hebrew Bible

The Hebrew or Jewish Bible (the Christian Old Testament) contains three main types of literature: narrative material including the Torah, prophetic books and books of wisdom, poetry and songs.

The books that make up the Hebrew Bible and, with key variations in order, the Old Testament were composed over a period of some 900 years. These books can be divided into three different kinds of writing and part of the fascination of biblical literature lies in this wide variety.

Narrative books

The first 17 books in the Jewish scriptures, from Genesis to Esther, are largely narrative. The first five of these books (Genesis, Exodus, Leviticus, Numbers and Deuteronomy) have a unique place in the Jewish scriptures. Together, they are known as the Torah (Law) or the Pentateuch and they contain the story of the exodus of the Jews from Egyptian slavery and their journey towards the Promised Land in Canaan. It was on this journey that the Israelites received their most precious gift from God, the Law. At the heart of this gift lay the Ten Commandments.

Prophetic books

These books are known as the 'Latter Prophets' in Jewish tradition; the 'Former Prophets' are the books of Joshua, Judges, Samuel and Kings. The Latter Prophets are the books of Isaiah, Jeremiah and Ezekiel (the 'Major Prophets') together with the 12 'Minor Prophets', from Hosea to Malachi. The Christian tradition includes the book of Daniel in the Latter Prophets as well. Although these books are named after a prophet, most of them were put together by disciples of the prophet rather than the prophet himself. Composed between the ninth century BCE and the third century BCE these books provide valuable historical information about very different periods in Israel's history.

Wisdom literature

This kind of literature includes the witty, pithy and instructional sayings that make

> Jesus said to them, 'This is what I told you while I was still with you: everything must be fulfilled that is written about me in the Law of Moses, the Prophets and the Psalms.' Then he opened their minds so they could understand the scriptures.
>
> LUKE 24:44–45

as Job and Ecclesiastes, tackle much weightier subjects, including the meaning and futility of life, evil and suffering.

Jesus recognized the existence of authentic Jewish scriptures when he referred to 'the Law and the Prophets'. Later Jewish writings also referred to the threefold division of the Law, the Prophets and the Writings. When Jesus appeared to his two disciples on the road to Emmaus after his resurrection he mentioned the Law of Moses, the Prophets and the psalms to them.

A Torah lesson from the Coburg Pentateuch. From a 14th-century Jewish manuscript illuminated in France.

up the book of Proverbs. The very nature of proverbs enabled people to remember them for a long time, and they ended up being passed down from generation to generation. Some wisdom books, however, such

The Septuagint

By the late fourth century BCE the Greek language had become the main tool of communication in much of the known world. In the Jewish communities widely dispersed across the Mediterranean and the Middle East few people spoke Hebrew, so whole communities were unable to read their own scriptures

I n a world dominated by Greek culture and language the need arose to translate the Hebrew scriptures into Greek. This work began in the third century BCE.

A Greek translation

A reliable Hebrew manuscript was sent from Jerusalem to Alexandria and Ptolemy II (282–246 BCE) commissioned the translation of the

The Pentateuch was translated from Hebrew into Greek in the city of Alexandria, Egypt. From a sixth-century mosaic in the Church of St John, Gerasa, Jordan.

Pentateuch (the first five books of the scriptures) into Greek. This translation, known as the Septuagint, continued with the remainder of the Hebrew scriptures over the following two centuries. Once the translation was complete two attitudes were taken towards it within Judaism:

◆ Some, especially among those Jews still living in Palestine, thought that the translation was too loose and undertook to revise it at a later date to bring it more into line with the Hebrew text.
◆ Others, among those living in the Diaspora, thought that the Greek translation itself was divinely inspired, thus giving the Septuagint an equal status with the Hebrew text. This group saw no need for any revision of the Septuagint, since it spoke with divine authority.

The value of the Septuagint
The Septuagint includes a number of writings which are not found in the traditional Hebrew scriptures, plus some translations from Aramaic originals and others composed in Greek. These became the basis for the Apocrypha, a collection of books from the inter-testamental period that is

accepted as canonical by the Roman Catholic and Eastern Orthodox Churches but not by Jews or Protestant Churches. So, for example, the books of Tobit, Judith, the Wisdom of Solomon, Sirach, Baruch, the Letter of Jeremiah, 1 and 2 Esdras and 1 and 2 Maccabees are included in the Septuagint but not in the Hebrew Bible. The Septuagint also abandoned the threefold division of the Hebrew Bible into Law, Prophets and Writings and there are marked differences in the order in which the books are listed.

The Septuagint had a considerable effect on early Christianity. As it was the main form of the Bible for Greek-speaking Jewish communities it was used by most of the early Christian communities as well. When the Jewish scriptures are quoted in the New Testament it is almost invariably from the Septuagint.

The Septuagint version of the Jewish scriptures took its name from the legend that this translation into Greek was undertaken by 70 (or 72) Jewish scholars and completed in as many days.

The Hebrew Canon

It is important to distinguish between the actual writing of the books in the Jewish Bible and their subsequent acceptance as scripture. For many of the books a long time elapsed between these two stages, although some were accepted far more quickly. A few were in doubt right up to the end.

The supremacy of the Pentateuch – the books of the Torah – for Jewish faith was recognized by the time of Ezra in the fifth century BCE, when many Jews drifted back to Israel from exile in Babylon. Some time after this the books of the Prophets, which included Joshua and the history books, became widely accepted, although the Samaritans, a despised offshoot of Judaism, did not accept them. The Samaritans only accepted the books of the Law as authoritative.

It was not until the first century CE that the Writings, made up of 11 books in Hebrew, were finally accepted as scripture, although this section of the Hebrew Bible has always been seen as subordinate to the Torah and the Prophets. The authenticity of the Writings was still in considerable doubt when it was debated by rabbis in the first few centuries CE. Other books were also debated vigorously for some time –

none more so than the book of Ezekiel – but none of them was removed from the final list.

Making the choice

Many factors contributed to the choice of certain books as scriptural, among them:

◆ the tradition that a book could be traced back to Moses. The books of the Pentateuch were called the 'books of Moses'.
◆ whether a book could be linked to one of the widely recognized Jewish prophets.

THE RABBIS OF JAMNIA

The rabbis who taught at Jamnia around 90 CE are widely credited with being responsible for the final choice of books in the Hebrew Bible. They excluded all those books that had been written in Greek and which were widely read by Greek-speaking Jews. These excluded books came to be known as the Apocrypha. It is noticeable, however, that the short epistle of Jude in the New Testament quotes from the apocryphal book of 1 Enoch as if it is quoting from the Hebrew scriptures.

From the fourth century CE the word 'canon', from the Greek word meaning a 'rule', was used to indicate those books which the Jewish community (and later the Christian Church) would accept as authoritative. They became the 'measure' by which truth and error could be judged.

Ezra writing the sacred books from memory in 458 BCE. From *Codex Amiatinus*, seventh century.

◆ whether a book carried a clear note of spiritual authority.

◆ whether a book was stored in the Temple in Jerusalem and therefore regarded as sacred.

Added to all this was the opinion of respected religious teachers and leaders.

The Dead Sea Scrolls

Documents first discovered accidentally in a cave on the edge of the Dead Sea in 1947 turned out to be the most important biblical archaeological discovery of the 20th century: the Dead Sea Scrolls.

The Dead Sea Scrolls are manuscripts, or fragments of manuscripts, thought to have been part of the library of a strictly ascetic Jewish community known as the Essenes who were based at Qumran and who buried the manuscripts before they were overrun by the Romans in about 68 CE. The Essenes then either scattered or were slaughtered. The find contains the oldest-known evidence for every book in the Hebrew scriptures apart from the book of Esther. The discovery also unearthed manuscripts of rules for community life, many previously unknown legal and mystical texts, and Jewish books not included in the scriptures.

One of the caves close to the site of the Qumran community in which the Dead Sea Scrolls were found.

Links with the New Testament

There are many parallels between the teachings of the Dead Sea Scrolls and those of the New Testament. This is important because many of these ideas were thought to have had a Greek origin, but their background can now be seen to be Jewish instead. The contrast between light and darkness, for instance, which is a feature of John's Gospel, is found in the scrolls. So, too, is the Christian idea of the Temple or the Church being a community of people rather than a building. The scrolls also look forward to a future in which the Messiah, a descendant of King David, leads his people to victory, preaches good news to the poor and raises the dead – a picture which bears a close resemblance to the mission of Jesus.

Some scholars think that John the Baptist may have been a member of the Qumran

One of the most exciting documents among the Dead Sea Scrolls is the Isaiah scroll. This scroll, consisting of 17 leather sheets sewn together, is about 1,000 years older than any other copy of Isaiah's prophecy. It was written about 900 years after the prophet himself lived.

The 'Temple Scroll' from Qumran.

Two Messiahs?

The leader of the community in Qumran was known as the 'Teacher of Righteousness' and he entered into correspondence with priests from the Jerusalem Temple. Under his direction the community, the 'Sons of Light', was awaiting the coming of the Messiah, a normal Jewish expectation. However, the Essenes of Qumran, unlike other Jews, were anticipating the arrival of two Messiahs: the 'Messiah of Aaron', a priest who would restore the true Temple in Jerusalem, and the 'Messiah of Israel', a righteous king who would deliver the nation from its enemies. In orthodox Jewish belief these two roles were combined in one person, just as they were by the early Church which believed Jesus to be the promised Messiah.

community. Some even suggest that Jesus himself was an Essene, pointing out that Jesus did, from time to time, encourage his followers to pursue the Essene spiritual values of self-denial, pacifism, the rejection of wealth and the sharing of property. However, the differences between the teachings of the Essenes, Jesus and the early Church are equally, if not more, significant.

By Word of Mouth

'Oral tradition' refers to material passed on from one generation to another by word of mouth. An extensive period of such transmission took place before the material was written down in the Old Testament. A much shorter time elapsed in the case of the New Testament.

Jesus, like many of the Jewish rabbis of his day, depended exclusively on oral teaching to communicate his message. The teaching of Jesus, and much of that of the early Church, was by word of mouth in Aramaic and Greek, the lingua franca of the day. People listened carefully and committed what they heard to trained memory. No early Christian writings in Aramaic have come down to us and it is unlikely that any ever existed. When the teachings of Jesus were first written down they had already been translated from Aramaic into Greek.

Oral tradition

This oral tradition had a long and distinguished pedigree. In ancient Israel pieces of poetry, stories and legends about heroes and songs of celebration circulated among the people long before they were written down. Accounts of momentous events such as the exodus and

The New Testament proclamation should take place by word of mouth, publicly in an animated tone, and should bring that forward into speech and hearing which before was hidden in the letters and apparent concealment... Christ himself did not write his own teaching as Moses did his, but gave it forth by word of mouth and commanded that it should be done orally.

MARTIN LUTHER (1485–1546), GERMAN MONK AND THEOLOGIAN, AND LEADER OF THE PROTESTANT REFORMATION

the wilderness wanderings were transmitted by one generation to another, gathering embellishments and adaptations along the way. This oral transmission preserved tradition while adding creativity and freshness. It was not until the 10th century BCE that the need to preserve tradition by writing it down was first appreciated.

The New Testament had

a similar but much shorter period during which stories about Jesus and the first Christians were passed from one person to another and from group to group, as the needs of preaching, teaching and controversy dictated. As a consequence much material that was not needed or used

For many centuries the only means of transmitting information to an illiterate community was by word of mouth. *The Arab Tale-Teller* by Emile Jean Horace Vernet (1789–1863).

simply perished. The material that survived passed through the modifications and re-interpretations that each situation demanded. The limit on this process was set, though, by the retentive memories of the people who were present at the original events and teachings.

During this time it appears that some material *was* written down before the records that we have in the Gospels. Sayings of Jesus were probably assembled and strung together and used by the early Christians and also by the writers of the Gospels, although it is not easy to be certain whether these traditions were oral or written. Matthew and Luke, for example, record parables and shorter sayings of Jesus in their Gospel accounts which could well have been taken from already existing written accounts. Material which Matthew and Luke share but which is not found in Mark's Gospel is said by scholars to have come from a hypothetical source which they call 'Q'. Mark, meanwhile, compiled his passion narrative of Jesus with great care. He prefaced it with a breathless account of the journeys of Jesus, the conflicts, the choice of disciples, the miracles and the parables. Mark also expounded and proclaimed the advent of the kingdom of God – for which he must have had access to his own sources, whether oral or written.

The New Testament

It took a long time for the Christian Church to decide which books should be included in the New Testament. Although the canon was largely settled by the middle of the fourth century it was still a matter of some debate for several more decades.

There were several steps towards the final recognition of the books to be included in the New Testament.

Stage one

The epistles sent to the various churches in the middle of the first century by the apostles were collected and circulated widely, while the letters of Paul were put together in a separate collection. The epistle to the Ephesians may have been an editorial introduction to this collection since it summarizes all of Paul's most important teachings.

Stage two

The oral traditions about Jesus were highly valued and, in due course, many of them were included in the four written Gospels. These works were frequently quoted from the middle of the second century onwards, indicating their pre-eminent status in the Christian community. Around this time Christians began to use the codex, which had an influence

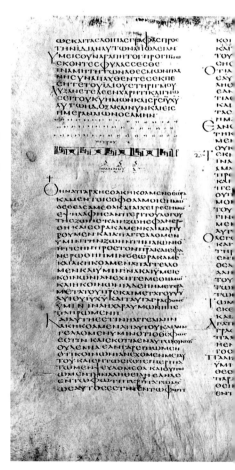

Codex Alexandrinus is one of the oldest copies of the Bible. Written in Greek, it dates from between 400 and 450 CE.

on the later canon: the four Gospels fitted conveniently into a single codex and this tended to eliminate rival accounts, of which there were many.

Stage three

The New Testament published by Marcion, a recognized heretic, in 140 CE contained most of Luke's Gospel and 10 epistles of Paul, unlike a larger collection of books which was already circulating widely in the Church. Forty years later Irenaeus, an important church leader, mentioned most of the later New Testament books and gave them equal authority with the books in the Jewish scriptures.

Stage four

The list of books in the Muratorian Fragment (c. 190 CE) included the four Gospels, the Acts of the Apostles, 13 epistles of Paul, the letters of John and Jude, and Revelation, but omitted Hebrews, James and the two epistles of Peter. Clement of Alexandria (died 215 CE) included Hebrews, while Eusebius (died 340 CE) was doubtful about the value of Revelation. Athanasius, a widely respected Eastern Church leader, listed the 27 books which were finally included in the New Testament and this

list was accepted by his Church as authoritative, as it was a few years later by the Western Church. The matter was finally settled in 397 by the Council of Carthage, which decreed that the reading of any but the 27 books in the canon was forbidden in public worship.

Making the final choice

The settling of an authorized canon was the Church's main defence against the often persuasive views of heretics. Among the criteria for deciding which books were to be canonical were:

◆ authorship by an apostle.
◆ the reliability of the book's witness to Jesus Christ.
◆ widespread agreement between the churches about the book's spiritual value.

At the time of the Reformation Martin Luther translated into German all the books of the Old and New Testaments, but relegated the books of the Apocrypha along with Jude, James, Hebrews and Revelation to an appendix. This precedent has not been followed by modern Lutheran Churches.

THE MAKING OF THE BIBLE

79

Translating the Scriptures

After early translations of the Bible into Greek and Latin the 16th century saw the beginning of the work of translation into English and the main languages of Europe and further afield.

Every translation of the Bible is an interpretation. There are no single original manuscripts to which translators try to return. Even the earliest available texts often allow several possible translations of single words, phrases or passages. Scholarship is continually opening up new possibilities. Translators always need to make judgments based on the available evidence. This is one reason why so many different translations have been made.

Early translations

Long before the canons of the Old and New Testament were agreed, translations were made into other languages. The most important were the Septuagint (from Hebrew to Greek), the Peshitta (from Hebrew into Syriac) and the Vulgate (from Hebrew into Latin). The Targums were translations from Hebrew into Aramaic.

Translations into English

The translation of the Bible into English owes a great deal to the work of William Tyndale (1494–1536). Competition between the Bishops' Bible and the Geneva Bible led King James I to commission the Authorized Version of the Bible, which appeared in 1611. The Revised Version, in 1881, attempted to update the Authorized Version, and the

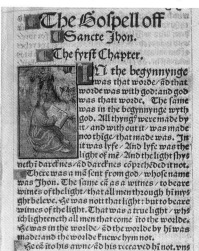

An edition of William Tyndale's New Testament, showing the opening of John's Gospel, with an illustration of the evangelist writing. Printed in Worms by Peter Schoeffer (c. 1525–26).

> *Whereas some men think translations make divisions in the faith, that is not so, for it was never better with the congregation of God than when every Church almost has a sundry translation. Would to God it had never been left off after the time of St Augustine, then we should never have come into such blindness and ignorance, such errors and delusions.*
>
> MILES COVERDALE (1488–1568),
> ENGLISH BIBLE TRANSLATOR

Revised Standard Version, in 1952, removed some archaisms. The Jerusalem Bible, for Roman Catholic use, was published in 1966, while the New English Bible, first published in 1961, was later revised as the Revised English Bible in 1989. The Good News Bible (1976) and the New International Version (1978) both proved to be extremely popular among Evangelical readers.

Other translations

By 1500 the Bible had been printed in four languages other than Hebrew and Greek: German, Italian, Catalan and Czech. In 1526 the first complete Dutch Bible was published, followed a few years later by its translation into Swedish. In 1551 the first Protestant translation of the Bible was made into Italian, although in 1564 Pope Pius IV forbade the use of the scriptures in the vernacular, effectively discouraging any further Bible translation until 1757.

The first printed Bible in French was published in 1530 and a new translation, with chapters and verses in place, came out in 1553. The definitive Geneva Bible in French was issued in 1588 and became the basis for many subsequent revisions. The first French Catholic Bible, published in 1550, also underwent many revisions. The first complete Spanish Bible, known as 'the Bear Bible', was published in 1569. Although the New Testament was first printed in Portuguese in 1681 a Portuguese Old Testament remained unpublished until 1751.

In Asia a flurry of Bible translations followed the 19th-century missionary movement. India has the Bible, or a part of it, in almost 150 languages or dialects. In Indonesia a part of the Bible exists in 74 languages or dialects, a process which began with the whole Bible in Javanese in 1854. Most of the languages of the Philippines had the complete Bible by the end of the first half of the 20th century. The first Bible in a Chinese dialect was published in 1823.

The Bible and the Reformation

The Bible was at the very heart of the Protestant Reformation and there was much agreement about it among the leaders of the movement, although there were some serious disagreements as well.

The Reformation was the religious movement in the 15th and 16th centuries which led to the formation of the Protestant Churches throughout Europe – especially the Lutheran and Reformed/Presbyterian Churches. The main Reformers on the Continent – Martin Luther, John Calvin and Ulrich Zwingli – agreed on the centrality of the Bible, the Word of God, although there were differences in the way that they understood it.

Ulrich Zwingli, the Reformer who clashed with Martin Luther over the interpretation of the wording of the Communion service.

Areas of agreement

During the Reformation, preaching and expounding the teachings of the Bible went hand in hand. A plaque in St Peter's Cathedral in Geneva honours John Calvin as 'the servant of the Word of God'. At the height of his powers Calvin preached an average of five sermons a week in the city, as well as delivering regular lectures which were later published in Latin. Luther, similarly, was totally committed to the preaching and teaching of the Bible.

The Reformers agreed that the Apocrypha was not part of scripture and Luther also rejected the epistle of James from the inner canon of scripture since it lacked 'explicit reference to Christ'. They taught that scripture was inspired in its original languages of Hebrew and Greek and that all Christian beliefs and traditions should be brought under its authority. At the same time it was fundamental to their teaching that the scriptures should be available in the vernacular of the people for everyone to read for themselves.

The Bible was central to Luther's theology, taking precedence for him over the traditions of the Church. *Portrait of Luther* by Lucas Cranach (1472–1553).

Areas of disagreement

A serious disagreement between Luther and Zwingli over Communion surfaced at Marburg in 1529. It revolved around the meaning of the words 'This is my body'. Should these important words be taken literally, as Luther

All I have done is to put forth, preach and write the Word of God, and apart from this I have done nothing. While I have been sleeping, or drinking Wittenburg beer... it is the Word which has done great things... I have done nothing: the Word has done and achieved everything.

MARTIN LUTHER (1485–1546), GERMAN MONK AND THEOLOGIAN, AND LEADER OF THE PROTESTANT REFORMATION

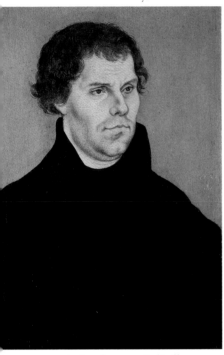

insisted, or symbolically, as Zwingli taught? This disagreement was more than a little embarrassing because Zwingli had previously argued, in *The Clarity and Certainty of the Word of God*, that the scriptures

carried their own clarity; this altercation seriously undermined that argument.

The Reformers also disagreed over the relationship between the Old and New Testaments. Luther was much keener than Calvin to find the New Testament teachings about Christ, the Trinity and the Church anticipated in the Old Testament. Calvin regarded the Old Testament Law as intrinsically valuable and part of God's unfolding revelation, while Luther believed its only real function was to convict people of sin, pointing to the grace of the gospel that Jesus came to bring.

Biblical Criticism

Biblical criticism means the examination of the books of the Bible using the tools which are provided by historical investigation, archaeology, palaeontology and linguistics. It starts from the premise that the Bible is a collection of books, of different kinds and written for various purposes by known, and often unknown, authors. The biblical critic uses the tools available to shed light on what the original authors were trying to say.

Although it is often painted in a negative light, biblical criticism is a necessary activity.

The Old Testament

The biblical critic deals with such questions as authorship, the date of writing, the contribution of later editors to the text and doctrinal tendencies and influences which can be seen in the text. The earliest biblical critics, in the 17th century, were Roman Catholic scholars such as Jean Astruc, who noticed that the

Charles Darwin (1809–92), whose theory of evolution presented a challenge to the biblical tenet of a divine creation. Photograph by Julia Margaret Cameron (1815–79).

book of Genesis was a compilation of several earlier documents rather than one book. The classical critical approach to the Old Testament was established in the 19th century by Graf and Wellhausen when they demonstrated that the books of the Pentateuch could not have been written by Moses, as was commonly supposed. At the same time, archaeology was showing the

> Biblical criticism has proved to be a dynamic field of study. New approaches and perspectives continue to appear... Serious work on scripture can be done only in continuity with the tradition of biblical criticism.
>
> JAMES BARR, PROTESTANT OLD TESTAMENT SCHOLAR

similarity between the religion of the Israelites and that of other cultures, while Charles Darwin was developing the theory of evolution which many

The findings of archaeologists have contributed to our under-standing of the cultural and historical context of the Bible. Excavating the Basilica of St Pachomius on the banks of the Upper Nile.

FORM CRITICISM

In the 1920s and 1930s several German scholars became increasingly frustrated with source criticism and sought to find out how material had been shaped in the years when it circulated by word of mouth in the early Christian community. It was suggested that the parables and miracles, in particular, arose out of a particular life-setting (the *Sitz im Leben*) – a kind of 'form' which followed patterns which could be deduced from the material we have today in the Gospels. This approach became known as form criticism.

took to show that divine creation and biological evolution were incompatible.

Source criticism

Similar investigation of the New Testament – especially the Gospels – followed. Everyone could see that the Synoptic Gospels had a great deal of material in common, but how did it happen? Who copied from who? Did each Gospel make use of another, common source? The examination of the relationship between them became known as source criticism.

Recent criticism has tended to concentrate on the Bible as literature. Rather than trying to reconstruct the historical development of the text, emphasis has been placed on the styles and narrative techniques of the text. The Bible must be understood by what is in the text – not by what is outside.

Judaism and Christianity are the only religions that share a substantial portion of their scriptures, although their attitudes towards them are very different.

Although Jews believe that the whole of their scriptures are inspired by God, it is the first five books, the Torah or Pentateuch, that are the foundations of their faith. Although the Sabbath day is a gift from God for which all Jews are eternally thankful, the Torah is the supreme gift from God to his people. As the Mishnah, a rabbinic commentary on the Torah, insists, the whole world is indebted to the person who studies the Torah. The Prophets and the Writings combine with the Torah to make up the Jewish scriptures.

Christians believe that the value of the Old Testament lies not so much in its intrinsic worth, as Jews believe, but in how it points to the coming of Jesus into the world. This event, known to

Murals of scenes from the Old Testament decorate the walls of a synagogue at Dura Europus, Syria, c. 200 BCE.

Christians as the incarnation, is explored by the four Gospels and forms the background to the Acts of the Apostles and the many letters found in the New Testament. Indeed all the books in the New Testament are an exploration of the central tenet of the Christian faith: that God entered the world in the form of Jesus of Nazareth, who lived on earth, was crucified and raised from the dead.

> *I have found in the Bible words for my inmost thoughts, songs for my joy, utterance for my hidden griefs and pleadings for my shame and feebleness.*
>
> SAMUEL TAYLOR COLERIDGE (1772–1834), ENGLISH POET AND LITERARY CRITIC

THROUGH THE BIBLE

Contents

The Five Books of Moses

The Torah, the opening five books of the Bible, is highly cherished within the Jewish community because it describes the creative activity of God in the world, the birth of the Jewish people and the giving of the precious Law on Mount Sinai.

The Torah, or *Chumash* (Hebrew for 'five', referring to the five books of Moses) was traditionally believed to have been written by Moses himself. Jews regard Moses as their greatest prophet. These same books are also known as the Pentateuch, from the Greek for 'five books'.

Genesis

The Greek word *genesis* and its Hebrew equivalent *beresit* mean 'beginnings'. Originally, Genesis was called the Book of Creation because it opens with an account of the creation of the universe. It also contains stories about the first man and woman, Noah and the great flood and the beginning of the Jewish nation, from Abraham and Sarah to Joseph and his family in Egypt.

> He who studies the Torah in order to learn and do God's will will acquire many merits; and not only that, but the whole world is indebted to him. He is cherished as a friend, a lover of God and of his fellow men.
>
> THE MISHNAH

An illustration of Noah's ark from the Caedmon manuscript, Canterbury, c. 1000.

MOSES

An ancient Jewish story tells how Moses, a shepherd, noticed that a young lamb was missing from his flock. He began to search for the animal and eventually found it, tired and thirsty. He gave it some water and carried it back to the flock. God saw this and said, 'If this man can show such love for one little creature, he deserves to be the leader of my flock, the people of Israel, as he will show them the same kindness and love.'

Exodus

The second book in the Torah, *Shemot*, meaning 'names' in Hebrew, was originally known as the Book of Going Out of Egypt. It tells the story of the slavery of the Jewish people in Egypt and of their final liberation under Moses and Joshua.

Leviticus

The third book of the Torah, *Vayikra*, meaning 'he called' in Hebrew, was first known as the Law of the Priests because it contains laws about animal sacrifices. However, its primary theme is that of holiness: the Jewish people are urged to be holy because God is holy.

Numbers

This book, *Bemidbar*, meaning 'in the wilderness' in Hebrew, was known as the Fifth of the Musterings, or gatherings, since it contains a census, a numbering of the Jews. It also describes the special role of the Levites, the deaths of Aaron and Miriam, the secret mission of the spies and the non-Jewish prophet, Balaam, with his talking donkey.

Deuteronomy

The earliest name for this book was the Repetition of the Torah, since much of the book repeats what is said elsewhere. The Ten Commandments, for instance, are recorded in Exodus and repeated in a slightly different form in Deuteronomy. The book ends with the farewell message and blessing of Moses before he dies.

Reading the Torah

Each week in the synagogue a section of the Torah is read to the congregation. The annual cycle of readings begins with Genesis and ends with Deuteronomy. These books are popular with Jews because they tell the stories of people with similar experiences and feelings to their own.

The Writing of the Torah

Moses was traditionally believed to be the author of the five books of the Torah, but it is now known that they did not have a single author, but probably came from four sources and were later arranged in their present form.

Scholars believe that the frequent duplication of material in the five books makes a single author most unlikely. In addition, these duplications each have a different vocabulary and a different style, for example, they regularly use different names for God. In the light of this overwhelming evidence scholars agree that the Torah is an amalgamation of four sources, which are rooted in the exodus event of which they speak, but were not written down for many centuries after Moses had died and probably were not in the form known to us until around 350 BCE. Let's look at these four sources in more detail.

Yahwist (J)

This source gives God the name of 'Yahweh' throughout. Most of the colourful and dramatic stories in the Torah come from J. The writer is concerned to show that God is approachable: at various times God is depicted as potter, gardener, householder, surgeon, tailor and judge. Yahweh does not tolerate any rivals but sympathizes with human weakness. The optimism of the J passages suggests that they date from the early days of Israel's monarchy, around 950 BCE.

Elohist (E)

This source prefers to call God 'Elohim', a plural of majesty and transcendance. When this God speaks to human beings, as Moses found, the ground itself

> *All the people had been weeping as they listened to the words of the Law. Nehemiah said, 'Go and enjoy choice food and sweet drinks... This day is sacred to our Lord. Do not grieve, for the joy of the Lord is your strength.'... Then all the people went away to eat and drink... and to celebrate with great joy, because they now understood the words that had been made known to them.*
>
> NEHEMIAH 8:9–10, 12

becomes holy and sacred. 'Elohim' could not at first be expressed in human language: when his name was first revealed to Moses it was translated as the 'Unapproachable Mystery'.

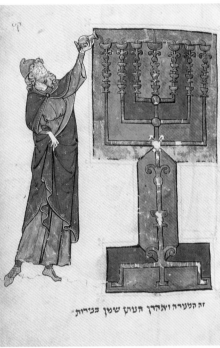

זה המערה ואהרן הטץ שמן בנרות

The High Priest Aaron Lighting the Menorah from a Jewish illuminated manuscript from Northern France, late 13th century.

The pessimistic tone found in E suggests the early ninth- and eighth-century BCE prophets and their fight against pagan encroachment on Israel.

Deuteronomist (D)

This source, found almost exclusively in the book of Deuteronomy, contains legislation but no stories. Yet, in a way, D tells a love story: God chose Israel out of pure love and Israel must love God in return by keeping his Law. To keep the Law fully the Israelites must love God, love their neighbour and love the stranger in their midst. The most significant piece of legislation in D is the restriction of worship in Israel to one single sanctuary, whereas J and E allowed many. This source has been dated to around 700 BCE.

Priestly (P)

The priestly tradition is so called because it concerns itself almost exclusively with liturgy, priesthood and worship. Its tone is dry, cold and technical. It tells the story of Israel from Adam onwards but in terms of a community bound to God through successive covenants – with Adam, with Noah and with Abraham. The priestly emphasis is on the holiness of God: 'Be holy, for I, Yahweh your God, am holy.'

The Former Prophets

The Prophets form the largest section of the Hebrew scriptures. The section takes its name from the political and religious activists who sought to call the nation back to its true and faithful belief in God and it is divided into two: the Former Prophets and the Latter Prophets.

The Former Prophets include the books of Joshua, Judges, 1 and 2 Samuel and 1 and 2 Kings. These appear to be straightforward historical books relating to the history of the Jewish people from the exodus out of Egypt to the time in the sixth century BCE when the nation of Israel was overrun by the Babylonians and thousands taken into exile. We also read of how, under kings David and Solomon, Israel enjoyed a brief period of stability and expansion. Most of the narrative, however, describes how the kingdom of Israel broke into two separate kingdoms, Israel and Judah, after the death of Solomon. Both of these kingdoms struggled to keep their independence, but Israel succumbed to Assyria in 722 BCE and Judah was overcome by Babylon in 586 BCE.

Prophecy not history
The Christian Bible may treat the Former Prophets as history but in the Hebrew Bible, according to tradition, they were treated as works of

prophecy. They were attributed to early prophets: Joshua (Joshua); Samuel (Judges, 1 and 2 Samuel); and Jeremiah (1 and 2 Kings). They share the prophetic characteristic of not only describing history, but also seeking to interpret it – and that is the main role of the prophet in any society.

The first king of Israel was Saul, who was followed by David and then Solomon. The rule of these three kings is referred to as the united monarchy. Soon after the death of Solomon the kingdom was divided into the southern kingdom of Judah and the northern kingdom of Israel. Judah consisted only of the tribes of Judah and Benjamin; the remaining 10 tribes made up Israel.

The future King David being anointed by Samuel and another figure, possibly David's father, Jesse. From a 14th-century English psalter.

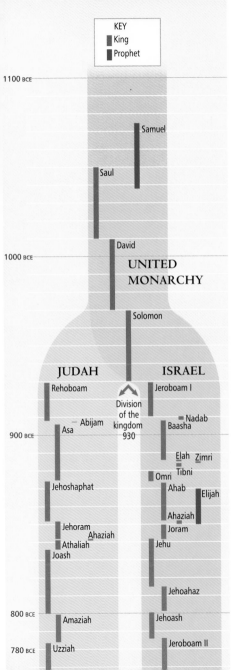

KEY
- King
- Prophet

1100 BCE

Samuel

Saul

1000 BCE

David

UNITED MONARCHY

Solomon

JUDAH   **ISRAEL**

Rehoboam   Jeroboam I

Division of the kingdom 930

Abijam   Nadab
Baasha

900 BCE   Asa

Elah   Zimri
Tibni
Omri

Jehoshaphat   Ahab   Elijah

Ahaziah
Jehoram   Joram
Ahaziah
Athaliah   Jehu
Joash

Jehoahaz

800 BCE   Amaziah   Jehoash

780 BCE   Uzziah   Jeroboam II

The writers of these books certainly sought to bring the eye of the prophet to contemporary history. They related the events of history to the relationship that the people had with God – a Chosen People called to be different from all the surrounding nations. Whenever the people remained faithful, worshipped as they were told by God and sought to follow his Law, they prospered. When they ignored God's command to walk in the ways of love and justice, they suffered.

Much of this story centres around the activities of Israel's leaders – mainly its kings. The good ones, such as Josiah and David, led the people into God-given peace and prosperity, while evil kings, such as Ahab, led the people into suffering and defeat. By discerning the will of God it is possible to understand just how one should live. That is the message of the Former Prophets.

The Major Prophets

The Latter Prophets fall naturally into two parts: the Major Prophets and the Minor Prophets. The Latter Prophets once circulated on a single scroll and come from the period between 750 and 350 BCE.

In the narrow sense of the word a prophet is someone whose name has been attached to one of the Old Testament prophetic books. There are three Major Prophets in the Hebrew scriptures.

Isaiah

Isaiah was an eighth-century BCE prophet.

Although some of the prophecies in the book bearing his name originated from the prophet himself, the book of Isaiah is now widely believed to have had three authors, the latest writing in the fifth century BCE. The first 39 chapters are the oldest in the book and it is these that are believed to

The Prophet Isaiah by Simone Martini (1284–1344).

have come from Isaiah himself. These chapters contain political and spiritual prophecies in which the author looks forward to the downfall of the kingdoms of Assyria and Babylon and foresees God's future kingdom of peace under the rule of the Messiah. Chapters 40–55 are prophecies of freedom from the Babylonian exile and the restoration of Zion, while the final chapters contain spiritual prophecies.

Jeremiah

Jeremiah lived at the end of the seventh century BCE. Much of the book of Jeremiah came from the prophet himself, although some of it may have come from the pen of Baruch, the prophet's amanuensis, with editorial additions by later scribes. The ministry of Jeremiah lasted for some 40 years, spread over the reigns of five monarchs, and he witnessed the fall of the city of Jerusalem to the Babylonians in 586 BCE. His personality – melancholic, depressive, sensitive and deeply emotional – shines more clearly through his work than that of any other prophet.

Ezekiel

Ezekiel is believed to have been the author of most of the book that bears his name and this dates from the end of the sixth century BCE. Ezekiel was among those Jewish leaders deported to Babylon after the fall of Jerusalem in 586 BCE and his prophetic message was directed to the exiles in Babylon. Somewhat surprisingly, he encouraged them to settle down and make themselves at home in their new surroundings. Apart from the message of judgment and the need for repentance, the book is marked by its emphasis on ritual and its descriptions of the prophet's visions. These include the famous vision of the dry bones which God miraculously brings to life. This introduced an element of apocalyptic imagery which is not found in the other Major Prophets.

The Minor Prophets

There are 12 so-called Minor Prophets in the Hebrew
scriptures and their books appear at the end of the
Old Testament in the Christian Bible. These prophets
preached the same message as Isaiah, Jeremiah and Ezekiel.

The books of the Minor
Prophets were written
between the eighth and the fourth
centuries BCE. They give little
biographical information and
consist mainly of the words of the
prophets whose names they bear.

From Hosea to Obadiah

The book of Hosea
dates from the end of
the eighth century BCE
and describes how God
instructed Hosea to
marry and remain true
to his unfaithful wife,
Gomer. The prophet's
experience is an
allegory of God's love for a
sinful and idolatrous Israel. The
book of Joel is probably from the
fifth century BCE, and describes
how a great plague of locusts
and its subsequent destruction
leads to his belief that God will
eventually restore and bless Israel.

Most of the book of Amos
dates from the eighth century
BCE and describes how the
judgment of God falls on Jewish
and Gentile people alike. Amos

Jonah emerges from the
mouth of the whale, while
God looks on. From an
English psalter, c. 1340.

is convinced that the twin sins
of empty religious ritual and the
oppression of the poor by the
rich are the reasons why Israel is
under divine judgment. Obadiah,
the shortest book in the Bible,
dates from the fifth century BCE
and describes the prophet's
expectation of Edom's
destruction and the
restoration of Zion.

From Jonah to Habakkuk

The date and
authorship of the book
of Jonah are uncertain,
but it was probably
written in either the
sixth or fifth centuries BCE. The
story of Jonah and his attempt
to escape from his prophetic

*The kingdom
of Israel came
to an end in
722 BCE, when
the Assyrians
sacked Samaria
and scattered
the population
of the country
throughout their
empire. Judah
survived until
the Babylonian
conquest and
destruction of
Jerusalem in
586 BCE. Those
Jews who were
exiled were
allowed to
return home by
the Persian king
Cyrus in 539 BCE,
following his
conquest of
Babylon.*

> *They will beat their swords into ploughshares and
> their spears into pruning hooks. Nation will not take
> up sword against nation, nor will they train for war
> any more. Every man will sit under his own vine
> and under his own fig-tree, and no one will make
> them afraid, for the Lord Almighty has spoken.*
>
> MICAH 4:3–4

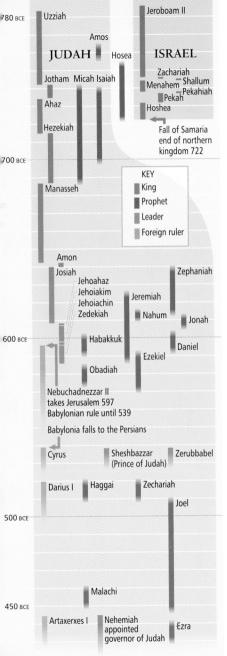

responsibilities shows God's loving care for everyone, including the people of Nineveh. Micah was a younger contemporary of the prophet Isaiah; he condemned corrupt rulers and priests and looked forward to a time of peace and prosperity for Israel. Micah foresaw the coming of the Messiah from Bethlehem. In the book of Nahum, from the seventh century BCE, the city of Nineveh is condemned for its idolatry, while in Habakkuk, from around the same time, God states that he will use the wicked Chaldeans to carry out his will.

From Zephaniah to Malachi

In a largely apocalyptic work Zephaniah prophesies the 'day of the Lord' on which divine judgment will fall on Judah, Jerusalem and various foreign nations. A 'remnant' of the people in Jerusalem will be saved and allowed to return from exile, an event celebrated by Haggai later in the fifth century. Much of Haggai's prophecy, as well as that of Zechariah, deals with the spiritual task of rebuilding the Temple. Malachi looks forward to the coming 'day of the Lord' when Israel would begin to enjoy God's blessings.

The Writings

The Writings, mostly poetical and wisdom literature, form the final section of the Hebrew scriptures.

The books in the Writings were the last to be written in the Hebrew scriptures. A few of them were nearly excluded from the canon of the scriptures because some people felt that they lacked divine inspiration. The Writings contain the following books: Ruth, 1 and 2 Chronicles, Ezra, Nehemiah, Esther, Job, Psalms, Proverbs, Ecclesiastes, Song of Songs, Lamentations and Daniel.

The wisdom books

In the Jewish scriptures wisdom is not as much an intellectual gift as a technical skill or the ability to live a satisfactory life. Above all, this wisdom is an attribute of God who created the world and gave Israel the Torah. This wisdom is usually personified as a woman or a sister.

The wisdom books in the Old Testament include Psalms, Proverbs, Job and Ecclesiastes. The teaching in these books is restrained and reasonable, depending more on human common sense than on the past history of Israel. Because

Where then does wisdom come from? Where does understanding dwell? It is hidden from the eyes of every living thing, concealed even from the birds of the air. Destruction and Death say, 'Only a rumour of it has reached our ears.' God understands the way to it and he alone knows where it dwells.

JOB 28:20–23

In places the Psalms include instructions to musicians and the names of tunes. Musicians with harps, a double pipe and hand drum from an Assyrian relief.

HEBREW POETRY

Poetry is not only found in the books of Psalms, Song of Songs and Lamentations, but also in many of the prophetic books. Most Hebrew poetry uses 'parallelism': the second line of a couplet repeats the idea in the first but in a different form. Sometimes the first line makes a positive point while the second line is negative. The book of Job is written in the form of a play, while Hebrew poetry also used riddles, parables and acrostics. In Psalm 119, the longest psalm, each stanza or section begins with a different letter of the alphabet.

Solomon acquired a reputation for wisdom, Proverbs and Ecclesiastes were associated with his name, although there is nothing else to link them with him. In fact, it seems likely that these collections of wisdom sayings were put together by groups who were trained in the traditional wisdom culture, as were similar groups in Egypt and elsewhere. The marked differences between rich and poor, the advantaged and the disadvantaged, all over the Near East led to the pithy observations about life contained in wisdom literature.

The two books of Job and Ecclesiastes have a stronger theological content than the other wisdom literature. At the time of the exile the old structures of cult, court and Temple broke down and it is likely that these books were put together to fill the resulting vacuum. Wisdom literature had a universal relevance and a practical role.

The Apocrypha

The word 'apocrypha' is taken from the Greek word meaning 'hidden things' and is applied to those books which are placed between the Old and New Testaments in many Christian Bibles.

Although the collection of books known as the Apocrypha is not included in the Jewish canon, some of the books were included in the Septuagint and in Jerome's Vulgate.

1 and 2 Esdras

The first of these books gives a parallel account of the history recorded in the books of Chronicles, Ezra and Nehemiah. The second describes seven visions in which Ezra enquires why God's people have to suffer and is told that such matters are incomprehensible to human beings. Ezra is assured that salvation is near and the Jews will, in the end, inherit the earth.

Tobit

This highly fanciful story takes place during the Babylonian exile and tells the story of a blind captive who is punished for burying the Hebrew dead – a solemn spiritual responsibility. His son, Tobias, falls in love with his cousin, whose previous seven husbands had been killed by the demon Asmodeus. Tobias, helped by the archangel Raphael, defeats the demon and restores Tobit's sight by means of a fish he has caught in the River Tigris.

Judith

This story from the second century BCE is about a beautiful Jewish widow whose city is besieged by Nebuchadnezzar's forces. She visits the Babylonian general's tent and cuts off his head when he falls into a drunken stupor. The city is saved.

There is no reference in Jewish literature to the Apocrypha as a collection of books, although there is a brief mention of 'outside books' (*Hishonim*), which may be an oblique reference to the apocryphal books.

THE CHRISTIAN BIBLE AND THE APOCRYPHA

The books of the Apocrypha are called deutero-canonical ('second-level') by Roman Catholics to distinguish them from protocanonical ('first-level') books in the canon. They are nonetheless regarded as authoritative and included in the Old Testament. At the time of the Reformation the Church of England reverted to the shorter Hebrew canon because it saw traces of the doctrine of purgatory and justification by works in apocryphal books.

Judith saves her city by beheading the Babylonian general who is besieging it. *Judith and Holofernes* by Michelangelo Merisi da Caravaggio (1571–1610).

Wisdom of Solomon

This book by an unknown author praises wisdom and exhorts everyone to seek it. The book discusses Jewish history and the way in which it has been helped by wisdom in the past.

Ecclesiasticus

This contains the wisdom sayings of Joshua ben Sira, who lived in Jerusalem around 180 BCE. The book recommends observing the Law and maintaining a pious fear of God. Ecclesiasticus was well regarded by both Jews and early Christians.

Baruch

Supposed to be the work of Baruch, the amanuensis of Jeremiah, this book begins with a prayer of confession, asking for repentance and salvation. The remainder is a hymn of praise to wisdom and a lament for the exiles in Babylon.

1 and 2 Maccabees

These books are concerned with Jewish history between 175 and 134 BCE and the heroic family of the Maccabees, especially Judas Maccabeus. It describes the struggles against the Syrian king Antiochus IV Epiphanes.

The Four Gospels

The four Gospels were not the first books in the New Testament to be written, since all of Paul's epistles pre-date them. Neither are the Gospels straightforward biographies of Jesus. They were written to proclaim the message of the early Church: that God's plan for the world and its salvation had been brought to fruition through the life, teaching, death and resurrection of Jesus.

The Gospels of Matthew, Mark and Luke have many similarities and are called Synoptic Gospels. New Testament scholarship has attempted to discover how these Gospels came to be written.

The message of the Gospels

Each of the Gospels is an interpretation, a picture, of Jesus and his message. As we read the Gospels we see Jesus through the eyes of the four evangelists, Matthew, Mark, Luke and John. Nevertheless, the picture they paint of Jesus is coherent and consistent. They all speak of a carpenter from Galilee who called himself the Son of man; who took Palestine by storm for a few short years through his preaching; who told parable after parable to teach the people about God's kingdom; and who underlined the truth of his preaching by the miracles he performed.

Jesus' popularity with the people brought him into direct conflict with the religious authorities – represented by the Pharisees, Sadducees and scribes – and it was this that led to him being condemned to death by the Roman occupational forces. Three days later, though, it was reported that Jesus had risen from the dead and the truth of this began to dawn on his first followers. The early Church began to proclaim that he was the Messiah, the Son of God. The Gospels became part of the Church's attempt to present the good news about Jesus throughout the Roman empire.

The Synoptic problem

As we shall see, the relationship between the four Gospels is rather complex. Three of them – Matthew, Mark and Luke – are known as the

Synoptic ('seeing together') Gospels because of their remarkable similarity to each other. While 90 per cent of John's Gospel has no parallel elsewhere, only 25 per cent of Matthew and Luke are peculiar to their own Gospel and Mark less than 10 per cent. The relationship between these three Gospels is known as the Synoptic problem.

The solution to the Synoptic problem depends on the strong probability that Mark's Gospel was the first to be written – around 65 CE. If so, both Matthew and Luke used Mark as one of their sources, independently of each other. This explains the material that all three have in common. Matthew and Luke have material in common which they do not share with Mark – scholars call this source 'Q' (from the German word *Quelle*, meaning 'source'). Matthew has material that no one else shares and this comes from his own source – called M. Likewise, Luke obtained information from his own source – L.

The setting of the Gospels is Judea and Galilee.

Matthew's Gospel

Throughout its history the Church has found Matthew's Gospel to be the most congenial and so it has been the one most frequently used in liturgy and worship. This may be because its interests seem to be more pastoral than theological.

A medieval view of the torments of hell. *The Last Judgment* by Hieronymus Bosch (c. 1450–1516).

Matthew's account is the most Jewish of the Gospels and it was widely held in the past, by St Augustine and others, that it was the first to be written: it is the first Gospel in the New Testament, and Mark's Gospel seems like a later abbreviation of it. The common view now, though, is that Mark's Gospel was the first to be written, in inelegant Greek, and that Matthew presented a much more polished Gospel for public consumption about 20 years later. In addition, Matthew includes a description of the birth of Jesus and much teaching of Jesus not found in Mark.

Matthew's characteristics and interests

The Jewishness of Matthew's Gospel is very clear. Matthew refers often to the 'kingdom of heaven' rather than the 'kingdom of God', a phrase found frequently in Mark and Luke, which demonstrates the traditional Jewish reluctance to

> *Blessed are the poor in spirit for*
> *theirs is the kingdom of heaven.*
> *Blessed are those who mourn,*
> *for they will be comforted.*
> *Blessed are the meek,*
> *for they will inherit the earth.*
> *Blessed are those who hunger*
> *and thirst for righteousness,*
> *for they will be filled.*
>
> MATTHEW 5:3–6

use the divine name. Matthew presents the teachings of Jesus in five blocks, each ending with the phrase, 'When Jesus had finished these sayings…' reflecting the five books of the Torah. The so-called Sermon on the Mount outlines the ethical standards expected of those who would enter the kingdom of heaven. The new 'law' of Jesus has superseded the old 'law' of Moses.

A prime concern of Matthew is to show how frequently events took place in fulfilment of prophecies made in the Jewish scriptures. His Gospel is an 'ecclesiastical' one, showing that the kingdom of heaven was beginning to be understood as the Church by the time that Matthew wrote. It is Matthew alone who mentions 'the Church' in connection with Peter as the Rock. Matthew also mentions the future expectation of judgment and the end of the world.

JESUS IN MATTHEW'S GOSPEL

Jesus frequently identifies himself as the 'Son of man' (a phrase used in the book of Daniel), while the demons recognize him as the 'Son of God' – Matthew's favourite title for Jesus. In the story of Jesus' passion there are several distinctive Matthean touches: the wife of Pontius Pilate intervenes; Pilate washes his hands to express his belief in the innocence of Jesus; and he hands Jesus over to the Jews. Their glad acceptance of responsibility for the death of Jesus has often been an excuse for Christian anti-Semitism. In Matthew's Gospel, Jesus is not taken by surprise by anything that happens to him; indeed, he warns his disciples of what is to come and he is perfectly aware of who will betray him.

Mark's Gospel

Mark's Gospel almost certainly gives us our earliest-known record of the life and teachings of Jesus. From the outset, Mark's life of Jesus moves quickly towards death and resurrection.

Mark is the shortest of the four Gospels. Both Matthew and Luke later used Mark as their main source of information. Traditionally ascribed to John Mark, the companion of Peter, this led to an early bishop, Papias, recording that Mark wrote down 'accurately but not in order', the recollections of Peter.

The themes of Mark

Mark used a number of existing short stories about Jesus and strung them together, sometimes quite haphazardly, since there is no attempt in the Gospel to be chronological. The main theme of the work is that of the suffering Messiah who made enemies because of his claims to be divine. The shadow of

THE ABRUPT ENDING

There are some unexplained puzzles associated with the way that Mark brings his Gospel to a climax with the death and resurrection of Jesus. There is the chilling and sinister depth of the cry of dereliction from Jesus on the cross; the unexpected darkness which covers the face of the earth as Jesus dies; and the abrupt ending to the Gospel with the fear of the women and their disobedient silence. The existence of both the Church and the Gospel itself implies that they were not silent for long. Mark's sentence about the empty tomb shows his own belief in the vindication of Jesus, brought back to life by God.

Yet it is the very suddenness with which Mark ends his Gospel that has caused endless speculation. There is another ending in some manuscripts, but this was probably written in the second century CE. It is possible, of course, that Mark did supply an ending which became detached from the Gospel for some reason at an early stage. Otherwise we can only guess at why the Gospel ends where and when it does.

The shadow of the cross falls across Mark's Gospel from the outset. *Christ on the Cross* by Ferdinand-Victor-Eugène Delacroix (1798–1863).

Anyone who wants to be a follower of mine must renounce self; he must take up his cross and follow me. Whoever wants to save his life will lose it, but whoever loses his life for my sake and for the gospel's will save it.

MARK 8:34–35

the cross falls across the Gospel from beginning to end. Jesus is the mysterious Son of God who is seen to be pressing on towards Jerusalem and death from the outset. Three times Jesus looks ahead to his own death and each time he invites his disciples to share in his 'cup of suffering'. Without doubt Mark was writing against the background of the Church's first real experience of persecution and was hoping to encourage it to persevere.

A secondary theme in the Gospel is that the Church is the legitimate successor to Israel in the purposes of God. This may account for his repeated use of the number 12: 12 disciples, 12 years of suffering for the haemorrhaging woman, the 12-year-old girl brought back to life and 12 baskets of leftovers after the feeding of the large crowd – all of which are reminiscent of the 12 tribes on which the nation of Israel was built.

Luke's Gospel

Luke was a Gentile who wrote his Gospel for fellow non-Jews. He set out to show that the main concern of Jesus was for the poorest and most despised members of society and that God was now working out his purposes through the Church rather than the nation of Israel.

The third Gospel comes from the same hand as the Acts of the Apostles and is similarly dedicated to a high-ranking Roman official, Theophilus. In the prologue to the Gospel Luke warns his readers that he is not an eyewitness to the events he describes and so has to make use of secondary sources. One of these is Mark's Gospel, which he freely borrowed from.

The Church, the new Israel

The Gospel of Mark was probably too rough and that of Matthew too Semitic for presenting the Christian gospel to the Greek-speaking world,

It was by a simple word of command that Jesus restored the daughter of the synagogue ruler to life. *The Raising of Jairus' Daughter* (1871) by Ilya Efimovich Repin (1844–1930).

> *Love your enemies; do good to those who hate you; bless those who curse you… If anyone hits you on the cheek, offer the other also… Give to everyone who asks you; if anyone takes what is yours, do not demand it back.*
>
> LUKE 6:27–30

but Luke's orderly and educated approach was ideal. He was thorough in his research, sympathetic in his approach and universal in his outlook. Not surprisingly, it is from Luke's Gospel alone that we learn of Elizabeth, Anna the prophetess, the female followers of Jesus and the widow of Nain's only son who died at a tender age. All of the stories about Mary, the mother of Jesus, come from Luke; she plays no part at all in Mark's Gospel and is totally silent in Matthew's account. Without Luke we would know nothing of the prostitute who washed Jesus' feet with her tears and dried them with her hair; of the bandit who repented of his sins on the cross of Calvary; or of the last words of forgiveness that Jesus spoke from the cross. Luke alone gives us the parables of the prodigal son, the lost sheep and the lost coin, together with the Pharisee and the publican and Dives and Lazarus

– all of which convey a universal message.

This universal nature of the Christian message runs through Luke's Gospel from beginning to end. Jesus is the Saviour of all, who has come to break down all of the barriers which exist between God and humanity. He is the one who befriends the least and the lost, the despised and those without hope. Luke's understanding of Jesus is close to that of Paul, the church leader whom he accompanied on some of his journeys, and he certainly reflects the victory of Pauline theology in the Church.

In both Matthew's and Mark's Gospels the end of time, the *parousia*, is prominent. Luke, however, emphasizes the joy of living in the Spirit-filled community of the Church, rather than looking forward to the end of the world. Luke wants to encourage his readers to be ready for the end to come, at some unknown time, but not necessarily soon. Instead of the message to the people to repent, there is the demand that they should be daily imitators of Christ.

John's Gospel

The world inhabited by John in his Gospel is very different from that of the Synoptic writers. He shares little of his material with them and he brings a highly theological approach to the life of Jesus.

John's Gospel was written much later than the others, probably around 95 CE, and is a more profound study of the life of Jesus than that of the other Gospel-writers. Although its language is simple it is, beneath the surface, a searching study of the mystery of Christ. In one way, this makes John easier to read than the other Gospels. He makes quite explicit what the others merely imply – that a Gospel is not a biography of Jesus but an interpretation of his life and teaching.

John's unique Gospel

There are several ways in which the picture of Jesus that emerges from John's Gospel is very different from that found in the Synoptic Gospels.

The infancy narratives

While both Matthew and Luke record the birth of Jesus, John makes the theologically profound statement that Jesus was 'the Word [of God] made flesh'.

The miracles

Both the exorcisms and the healing of the lepers, so important to Mark, are missing from John, but he does include seven other miracles – including the changing of water into wine – which he calls 'signs'. While the miracles in the Synoptic Gospels were indications of the coming of God's kingdom, to John they showed that Jesus was the Son of God.

WHY DID JOHN WRITE?

Clement of Alexandria, writing towards the end of the second century CE, claimed that after the other three Gospels had been written John wrote 'a spiritual Gospel'. There is some truth in this. John states his aim in writing the Gospel as being: to help his readers come to believe that Jesus is God's Son and to allow his readers to share in that eternal life which is given to all who believe.

The ministry of Jesus

In the Synoptic Gospels most of the ministry of Jesus takes place in Galilee, whereas in John the action is centred on Jerusalem and revolves around the Jewish festival themes of light, life and glory. In John

Christ was furious to discover that his Father's house had been turned into a market. *Christ Driving the Traders from the Temple* by Bernardo Cavallino (1616–56).

> *In the beginning was the Word, and the Word was with God, and the Word was God. He was with God in the beginning. Through him all things were made; without him nothing was made that has been made. In him was life, and that life was the light of men. The light shines in the darkness, but the darkness has not understood it.*
>
> JOHN 1:1–5

allegorical form: Jesus calls himself the good shepherd; the door; the way, the truth and the life; and the bread of life.

We can safely assume that most of John's readers would have been familiar with the Synoptic accounts and so John set himself the task of gathering together the many fragments found in those Gospels to form some kind of integrated whole. This would prove enormously influential. John's Gospel provided the foundation on which much of the later understanding of Jesus was to be based.

the cleansing of the Temple is placed very early in the ministry of Jesus and there is no record of the transfiguration.

The teaching of Jesus

The teaching of Jesus in John lacks the short, pithy sayings and parables found elsewhere and consists, instead, of long discourses. Jesus' teaching about himself is often in

The Acts of the Apostles

The fifth book of the New Testament, the Acts of the Apostles, is our only real source of information about the early years of the Christian Church. It covers a period of about 30 years from the birth of the Church through to the imprisonment of Paul in Rome.

It would be impossible to write a history of the early Christian Church without the information provided by Acts. Peter, the disciple of Jesus, is the main character in the first part of the book and Paul, the converted Pharisee and persecutor of the early Christians, dominates the remainder.

The story of Acts

The Acts of the Apostles almost certainly had the same author as the Gospel of Luke and was probably written about the same time – during the seventh or eighth decade of the first century. It neatly takes up the narrative where the Gospel ends, adopts a similar style and displays the same humanitarian interests.

Acts charts the course of events which began on the Day of Pentecost when the Holy Spirit was given to the dispirited disciples, through to its abrupt, and somewhat surprising, conclusion with Paul under house-arrest in Rome. In between the story told is that of the Christian gospel moving through much of the Roman empire with great speed; a story of considerable success, some failure and much hardship. There is also internal dissent within the Christian community, particularly between those who favoured a universal Church open to all without any strings attached and those who wanted new converts to pay more than lip service to the Jewish background from which Christianity had sprung. The unity of the Church was maintained by an

> *You will receive power when the Holy Spirit comes on you; and you will be my witnesses in Jerusalem, and in all Judea and Samaria, and to the ends of the earth.*
>
> ACTS 1:8

directed by the Holy Spirit. God, through the Holy Spirit, occasionally altered the plans of the missionaries, diverting them from one path and into another, but that is the divine prerogative. Luke has often been called 'the theologian of salvation history' – Peter and Paul were the principal human agents, but the dominant part in bringing salvation to the masses was played by the Holy Spirit. This is why the Holy Spirit is mentioned no less than 57 times in this book.

Luke brings to a conclusion a story which in the first volume had begun and ended in Jerusalem, but which had acquired, by the end of the second volume, a worldwide relevance.

The Holy Spirit descends as fire on the disciples on the Day of Pentecost. Anglo-Saxon illustration from the Benedictional of Archbishop Robert.

unsatisfactory compromise which was cobbled together by Peter, Paul and others meeting in Jerusalem around 50 CE.

The Acts of the Holy Spirit

Just like the Gospel writers, Luke, in Acts, was no mere chronicler of events. He sees a consistent pattern in the events he describes. The gospel was launched on the world by the resurrection of Jesus and the gift of the Holy Spirit and nothing could halt its advance. Paul and the other apostles could plan their journeys but they would achieve little unless they were

The New Testament Letters

There are many letters or epistles in the New Testament, the majority of them written by Paul. The remainder are associated with other church leaders such as James, Peter and John.

Within a decade of the death of Christ thriving churches were to be found in all the major cities of the Roman empire. Many books in the New Testament were written to encourage these churches to understand the faith they had embraced. Most of them were letters sent by Christian leaders to their converts, often to answer specific questions and issues that were being raised in the Christian community.

Sending letters

Not everyone in the Roman empire or the Christian Church was literate, but letters were often read aloud to groups of people. Although the Romans had their own language of

Two authors of New Testament letters, the apostles Peter and Paul, portrayed in an unfinished relief from the fourth century CE.

> *I am convinced that neither death nor life, neither angels nor demons, neither the present nor the future, nor any powers, neither height nor depth, nor anything else in all creation, will be able to separate us from the love of God that is in Christ Jesus our Lord.*
>
> ROMANS 8:38–39

Latin, they conversed and conducted business in Greek, although in Palestine Greek was used alongside the local dialect of Aramaic. Most letters took a standard form: opening salutations were followed by the main body of the letter before closing greetings. The New Testament letters follow this pattern. Paul's letters, in particular, are of this kind. His letters adopt a very personal tone of the kind that would be used between friends. Four of the letters associated with his name were sent to individual Christians – Philemon, 1 and 2 Timothy and Titus – while the remainder were directed to churches.

Some of the other letters in the New Testament follow this formal style of letter-writing less closely and may not have been real letters. Instead they may have been attempts to set down a formal statement of the Church's teaching on important doctrinal matters. The letter that fits into this category most clearly is the epistle to the Hebrews, an anonymous work which, judging by its subject matter, must have been addressed to a community largely made up of Jewish converts to Christianity.

Using the letters

Whatever form the letters took we can guess that most of them were written to address particular areas of concern in the early Church, although there are often few clues about the exact nature of the problem. Certainly most of the letters written by the apostles were brought together and circulated widely almost as soon as they were written. Paul, we know, recommended that two of the churches to whom he had written should exchange the letters he sent them. By the time that 2 Peter was written, towards the end of the first century, Paul's letters had clearly been gathered together and placed alongside the Old Testament as sacred scripture. They were read in the course of regular worship.

The Letters of Paul

Paul's influence in the early Church was established by the visits he made to many Christian communities and the letters he wrote to them. Paul's letters explained Christian doctrine and encouraged young believers to remain faithful to the gospel message.

The letters traditionally thought to have been written by Paul fall naturally into four groups.

1 and 2 Thessalonians

These were probably the earliest letters written by Paul in around 49 CE. Paul had been a Christian for about 15 years and had spent much of that time teaching and establishing new churches around the Mediterranean area. In these two letters Paul recalls the time he had spent in Thessalonica, encourages the believers there to live a life of love and holiness and looks forward to the return of Christ.

Romans, 1 and 2 Corinthians and Galatians

The letter to the Romans, the longest of Paul's works, is the nearest we come to a full explanation of the Christian gospel. Paul's reason for writing this letter is not clear, since at the time he had not visited Rome, although he hoped to go soon. He wanted to bring about a reconciliation between Jewish and Christian groups in the city. Paul wrote his first letter to the church in Corinth in reply to a letter he had received from the Christians there. He wrote another letter to warn and encourage the Christians living in a particularly immoral city. Paul wrote the letter to the Galatians to counteract the false teaching that Gentile Christians needed to be circumcised and to keep the Jewish law.

Ephesians, Philippians, Colossians and Philemon

In these letters, known as the prison epistles, Paul mentions that he is a prisoner, probably in Rome. Ephesians contains teaching about Christ, the world and the Church. In his letter to the Christians in Philippi, Paul is thankful for the many kindnesses the church there had shown him and he encourages them to remain united and joyful in the face of opposition and threats. In Colossians Paul is concerned to

> *If God is for us, who can be against us? He who did not spare his own Son, but gave him up for us all — how will he not also, along with him, graciously give us all things? Who will bring any charge against those whom God has chosen? It is God who justifies.*
>
> ROMANS 8:31–33

combat false teaching which was threatening the church at Colosse. To Philemon Paul wrote a tactful letter seeking forgiveness for Onesimus, a runaway slave of Philemon, who has crossed the apostle's path.

that Paul wrote these letters, known as the pastoral epistles, towards the end of his life and, if so, he had probably been released from his imprisonment in Rome, with which the Acts of the Apostles closes. In the pastoral epistles Paul shows a deep concern for the welfare of his churches and speaks of his desire to know that they are in good hands. In 2 Timothy, written just before Paul's death, Paul encourages Timothy, a young pastor, to remain faithful to the Christian gospel which he has been taught from his childhood.

1 and 2 Timothy and Titus
Many people think it is likely

The ruins of the Temple of Apollo high above Corinth. The city stood at the crossroads of trade routes by both land and sea. It was a centre for the exchange of cultures and religions, but also had a reputation for immorality. Paul's two letters to the Corinthian Christians contain much practical advice on how to live in an ungodly world.

Other New Testament Letters

Alongside the letters associated with Paul's name, the early Christians were anxious to preserve a number of letters written by other church leaders. These letters are grouped together in the New Testament.

Of the remaining epistles in the New Testament one is anonymous (Hebrews); one was written by James, the brother of Jesus (James); two were linked to Peter (1 and 2 Peter); three were written by John (1, 2 and 3 John); and one was written by Jude, the brother of James.

Hebrews

This substantial letter was written to a group of Jewish Christians, possibly in Rome, who were separating themselves from the main Church and looking to find their spiritual home in Judaism. The unknown author was alarmed by this because he believed that all of God's purposes were now being channelled through Christ, the Jewish Messiah.

James

James, the brother of Jesus, was the leader of the Jerusalem Church. His epistle is probably

Emperor Nero, whose persecution of Christians in 64 CE was the first to be sanctioned by the state.

the earliest book in the New Testament, dating from the mid-40s CE, and it reflects an early period in Church history, when Jewish Christians still belonged to their local synagogues. In the letter, James these new Christians encourages them to be distinctive disciples for Jesus.

1 and 2 Peter

Both of these letters were sent to Christians scattered in five districts of Asia Minor. The first letter warns them of coming persecution and encourages them to remain faithful to Jesus, who won their salvation on the cross. The second letter warns against a false teaching circulating at the time that encouraged immoral behaviour. The second letter is unlikely to have come from Peter and may be later than any other writing in the New Testament, written around the turn of the first century CE.

The Colosseum in Rome provided entertainment for a capacity crowd of 70,000. Cruelty was applauded, and many people met their death in the arena. Towards the end of the first century, persecution of Christians was on the increase.

> *Dear friends, let us love one another, for love comes from God. Everyone who loves has been born of God and knows God. Whoever does not love does not know God because God is love. This is how God showed his love among us: he sent his one and only Son into the world that we might live through him. This is love: not that we loved God, but that he loved us and sent his Son as an atoning sacrifice for our sins.*
>
> 1 JOHN 4:7–10

1, 2 and 3 John

Written by the author of John's Gospel, these three epistles were probably composed in the last decade of the first century CE. Fighting against a teaching that a remote God could only be reached by some superior intellectual insight, which had no link with the behaviour of the body, John insisted that Christ was unique and that a faith which did not result in a holy life was useless. God is love; this love has taken on human form in the life of Jesus, and Christians, united to God in Christ, must express their faith by a holiness and love for others which reflect the holiness and love of God.

Jude

This epistle, written by the brother of James around 80 CE, was directed against a philosophy which tried to reduce Jesus to little more than a superior kind of angel.

THE CATHOLIC EPISTLES

James, 1 and 2 Peter, 1, 2 and 3 John and Jude are sometimes called the catholic or universal epistles because, with the exception of 2 and 3 John, they were intended for a general audience rather than a specific church or person.

119

Revelation

The book of Revelation describes a great vision given to John, possibly the author of the fourth Gospel, who was in exile on the isle of Patmos.

First composed around 95 CE the book of Revelation began as a letter sent to the different Christian communities in Asia Minor (as the first three chapters make clear). In one sense the book belongs to the group of universal or general epistles just considered, but its subject matter and style place it in a class of its own.

The book of Revelation

Whether or not Revelation was written by the author of John's Gospel there is a strong affinity of thought between the two books: in Jesus, God has made his final revelation to the human race. God will not say or do anything more. In the death and resurrection of Jesus, God has shown all that there is to be known about himself and completed the work of the world's salvation.

This was offered as a message of hope to the Christians of the first century who, through their suffering and persecution, were beginning to doubt whether God would ever finally defeat the powers of evil and destruction. The book of

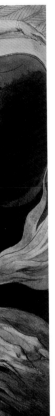

Revelation assures them that this final victory has already been won by God and that they share in it because of their persecution – not in spite of it. Their very suffering baptizes them into the death of Jesus and without this they cannot hope to share in the glory of his resurrection.

THE MESSAGE OF REVELATION

The book of Revelation is not quite the unfathomable mystery it is often made out to be. The author was not foretelling events far into the future although some, largely for dubious motives, have made this out to be the case. He was certainly not prophesying events which some have seen as taking place in the 20th and 21st centuries. His own readers saw them as reflecting the very events that they themselves were caught up in and in which which they were being asked to share in the death and resurrection of Jesus. As such, the book provided a profound message of encouragement to the Church at the time and in the future: through its suffering comes its final vindication and victory. Revelation provides a very suitable spiritual end to the Bible.

Apocalypse

This stirring and encouraging message is shared with Christians in the form of an apocalyptic discourse. For dramatic emphasis events contemporary with the author are described as if they had been revealed in visions experienced in the past. Under a number of different symbols – lion, lamb, Son of man, horseman – Jesus is pictured as being present in these contemporary events and through them gaining victory over the powers of evil, which are also presented in symbolic forms, such as dragon, beast, Babylon and sea. This victory does not simply come at the end of the book but at the end of each of seven separate tableaux – each complete in itself – between chapters 4 and 21.

The book of Revelation ends with a promise from Jesus: 'Yes, I am coming soon,' to which the author replies on behalf of his readers, 'Amen. Come, Lord Jesus.' He then adds to his readers, now as then, 'The grace of the Lord Jesus Christ be with God's people. Amen.'

The Bible is the most widely translated, printed, distributed and best-selling book of all time.

Those seeking to understand the Bible in the context of contemporary culture often struggle to find and explain its relevance in a world where relativism rather than any form of absolutism holds sway. Christians in many parts of the world have adopted a radical approach. In Latin America church leaders and lay Christians declared that Christianity offered a 'preferential option' for the poor based on Jesus' teachings in the Bible. In Africa the challenge has been to bring a distinctive cultural background to the study of the Bible to show that the two are not incompatible.

Elsewhere, the Bible has fuelled cultural advances in many different areas. For centuries the Church was the only serious sponsor of art, and there was an integral link between music

The Finding of Moses by Pharaoh's Daughter (1904) by Sir Lawrence Alma-Tadema (1836-1912).

nd the Church. The Bible has also
provided novelists, poets and dramatists
with a wealth of allusion and metaphor.

It looks likely that the Bible's
influence will increase in areas of the
developing world where Christianity is
expanding. More and more people will
have access to it, in electronic as well
as written forms. In the Western world,
however, the challenges to Christianity
and its holy book are considerable.

*Personal conversion and social
transformation are proposed in the Bible.
The reign of God is a utopian horizon, but
it also begins to be built here on earth.*

SERGIO TORRES,
LATIN AMERICAN THEOLOGIAN

THE IMPACT OF THE BIBLE

Contents

The Bible and Mission

During the past two centuries there has been a close link between the missionary work of the Church and the printing and distribution of the Bible by Bible societies in different countries.

Matthew's Gospel ends with Jesus commissioning his disciples to 'go and make disciples of all nations, baptizing them in the name of the Father and of the Son and of the Holy Spirit'. The Christian Church has taken this command with varying degrees of seriousness. Real missionary lift-off occurred in the early decades of the 19th century and it was soon realized that any lasting expansion of the Church would need to be accompanied by the widespread availability of the scriptures in the language of the people.

Taking the Word to the world

Kenneth Latourette, a leading church historian, labelled the 19th century as 'the great century', since it saw an unprecedented expansion of the Church throughout the world. Most of this expansion was led

In 1806 a group of students in Massachusetts gathered under a hay shelter during a rain-storm and prayed for a global missionary movement. They formed the Society of Brethren in 1808 but were more widely known as the Haystack Group. In 1810 they formed the American Board of Commissioners for Foreign Missions – the first American society dedicated to worldwide missionary work.

by Protestant Churches increasingly confident in the message that they had to proclaim. They founded many missionary societies and increasing sums of money were donated for their work. The Church Missionary Society, for instance, received about 3,000 pounds sterling in 1803 but this had topped 115,000 pounds sterling by 1843. The Anglican Society for the Propagation of the Gospel had been active in America since 1701 and this was followed by the Baptist Missionary Society (1792), the Church Missionary Society (1799) and the British and Foreign Bible Society (1804). In America the Board of Commissioners for Foreign Missions was founded in 1810, followed by the American Baptist Missionary Board four years later.

Because the Bible and mission were so closely linked there was a corresponding proliferation of Bible societies around the same time. The American Bible Society was founded in 1816 to provide Bibles for immigrants, Native Americans and others who could not afford or did not have access to the Bible for themselves. The British and Foreign Bible Society spawned a wave of similar Protestant and

> *To distance oneself [from the biblical text] means to be new to the text (to be a stranger, a first-time visitor to the text), to be amazed by everything, especially by those details that repeated readings have made seem so logical and natural. It is necessary to take up the Bible as a new book, a book that has never been heard or read before.*
>
> ELSA TAMEZ,
> MEXICAN METHODIST THEOLOGIAN

Catholic organizations in Scotland, Ireland, Australia, New Zealand, Russia, Germany, Holland, Norway, Sweden, Denmark and Canada. One or two of these, such as the Bible Society in Russia, were comparatively short-lived.

The collective work of these groups has continued down to the present time. With the resurgence of the Evangelicals within church life since the 1950s the link between the Bible and missionary enterprise became even closer. The British and Foreign Bible Society changed its name to the Bible Society but the motivation remained the same: to bring the scriptures to all people in their native language.

Copies of portions of the Bible are distributed from a truck in West Africa.

The Americas

Although America's involvement with the Bible has become much more diffuse in the 20th and 21st centuries, the Bible still constitutes a fundamental part of American-Christian experience.

During the 19th century the Bible was the most pervasive symbol of Christian America. America's fascination with the Bible, which continues today, has its roots in the Protestant Reformation, which took its own course in the country through the upsurge in democracy between the American Revolution (1775–83) and the American Civil War (1861–65).

Throughout its history, America has sustained an incredible rate of Bible production and an unceasing appetite for books explaining its meaning and message. Over 2,500 different English-language editions of the Bible were published between 1777 and 1955. Until well into the 20th century, the King James Version and the Douay-Rheims Catholic Bible overwhelmed all others. The American Standard Version of 1901 began to open up the market to new translations, and since then the New English Bible, the New American Bible, the Good News Bible and the New International Version have all enjoyed considerable success. Bible societies have strongly marketed the Bible.

Liberation theology

Liberation theology is closely

NATIVE AMERICA

By the beginning of the 21st century, at least one book of the Bible had been printed in each of 400 Native American languages. Fifty per cent of these languages now have the entire New Testament while 15 per cent have the whole Bible. This means that 98 per cent of Native Americans have at least a small part of the Bible available to them. Parts of the Bible have also been translated into seven Creole languages; the whole Bible has been translated into Haitian Creole. The availability of the Bible in these languages does not, however, guarantee that it is read since, among some groups, illiteracy is as high as 90 per cent.

Native Americans perform the White Buffalo dance in New Mexico.

> *The God we know through the Bible is a liberating God, a God who destroys myths and alienations, a God who intervenes in history to break down the structures of injustice and who raises up prophets to point the way to justice and mercy. He is the God who frees slaves, who makes empires fall and lifts up the oppressed.*
>
> BOLIVIAN METHODIST EVANGELICAL CHURCH CONFERENCE, 1970

Many Christians maintain that it is also natural that people should look to Christ and the Bible for a message of hope.

The discovery of such hope in the Bible has led in recent years to the formation of many base communities in Latin American countries – groups of laypeople who study the scriptures in order to gain an understanding of the reasons for oppression in their own country. By the end of the 1980s there were over 500,000 such base communities in Brazil alone.

Some figures in the Catholic Church in South America have been closely associated with the struggle to improve the living conditions of the poor. A priest in Columbia conducts Mass.

associated with the Church in Central and South America. It is a distinctive approach to the Bible which takes as its starting-point the communal experience of the poor and oppressed. It is natural that the poor should long to share in the wealth of those around them and that the oppressed should look for freedom from their oppressors.

Africa

Increasingly, the Bible has been translated and circulated throughout Africa, and led to many novel indigenous expressions of the Christian faith. Such expressions often have as much to do with the cultural and spiritual background of the worshippers as with the Bible.

The Bible has had a considerable effect upon Africa and Africa has had a great effect on the Bible. When the Bible was brought to Africa by colonizing missionaries in the 18th, 19th and 20th centuries it was often used as part of the economic and political oppression of indigenous Africans. In the decades that followed, Africans often retained the Bible by relativizing, resisting and modifying its message with considerable skill and creativity.

In their zeal to save the souls of Africans from eternal damnation, the early missionaries mixed Christian principles with Western culture, not to say beliefs... The god that was introduced to Africa was a completely foreign god, and this robbed Christianity of its universality.

AKIN J. OMOYAJOWO, NIGERIAN
BLACK THEOLOGIAN

Africa and the Bible

Some modern observers argue that African Christian scholars have dealt with the Bible on the basis of a transaction. Africans have not come to their study of the book empty-handed, but have brought to it their own cultural, social, political and religious experiences. In so doing they have found, for example, close similarities between their own worldviews and those expressed in both the Old and New Testaments.

This approach to the Bible is shared by scholar and ordinary Christian alike. Recent trends in scholarship – towards postmodernism and liberation readings of the text – go some way in the direction of the average African reader. Moreover, the distinctive contributions of African women to the reading of the Bible, stemming from their own experiences, are a factor of increasing importance, since women play a major role in

Bible translators in Tanzania involved in the painstaking task of making the scriptures available in another language.

many African churches. Everyone brings to the Bible their own distinctive cultural and social background, which means that the Bible cannot be understood in a European, and white, manner.

An oral knowledge

Africans also bring a strong oral knowledge to their reading of the Bible. This is especially true of young Christians in the African Independent Churches, who learn isolated verses from the Bible by heart, from conversion onwards, and incorporate them into their personal and ongoing spiritual experience. Often these converts carry a copy of the New Testament with them, so that they can ask a literate member of their congregation to read some verses to them.

They then commit the verses to memory.

The work of translating the Bible into the various languages and dialects of Africa has been a major part of missionary work in recent decades. It has now been translated into more than 230 African languages. One consequence of this widespread availability of the written text, together with a gradual growth in literacy among Africans, has been to weaken the European hold and open the way to the growth of new, indigenous forms of Christianity which may only be loosely linked with the Bible.

Europe

The continent of Europe has been deeply and lastingly affected by the Reformation and the Bible. The work and witness of the Catholic and Orthodox Churches have also been influential, although to a lesser extent.

In the 15th and 16th centuries the Reformation spread throughout Europe. It was firmly based on the Bible as the sole source of authority in the Church. The foundation for the movement was the translation of the Bible into a wide variety of European languages. The Reformation would have been impossible without the availability of the Bible in the vernacular language of the people.

Translating the Bible

By the end of the 14th century a complete New Testament (the Augsburg Bible, 1350) and Old Testament (Wenzel

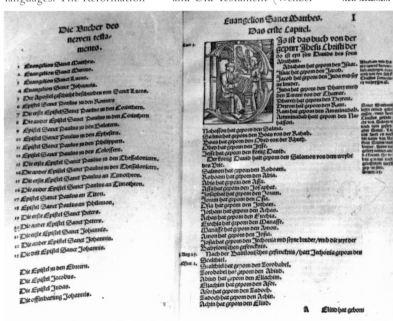

Martin Luther's New Testament

The teachings of the Bible have strongly influenced the Protestant Churches of Eastern Europe. A service in a Hungarian Reformed Church in Romania.

Bible, 1389–1400) were available for people to read in German. This translation and printing of the Bible lagged behind other European countries. When the first printed German Bible was published in 1466 it reflected the language and translation techniques of some 200 years earlier.

The earliest-surviving complete Bible in Italian dates from the early 15th century; it is in the Tuscan dialect and derives from the Latin Vulgate. The first complete Spanish translation of the Bible, the 'Bear Bible', was made in 1569 and this is still the standard Spanish Protestant Bible today.

A great step forward was taken as a result of the Reformation and the Renaissance. From the 16th to the 20th centuries new

> *May the sun on your rising find you with the Bible in your hand.*
>
> EVAGRIUS OF PONTUS (c. 305–400), DESERT HERMIT AND SPIRITUAL WRITER

manuscript discoveries enabled regular translations into German, French, Dutch, Swedish, Danish, Norwegian, Faroese, Italian, Spanish, Romanian, Slavonic, Bulgarian and other languages. These translations emanated from both the Protestant and Catholic wings of the Church. Sometimes the translations competed with each other in a bewildering fashion with little spirit of ecumenism.

The Bible and the Orthodox Church

The Orthodox Church has had an immense influence on Europe since its origins back in the fourth century. Like the Catholic Church, with which it has many similarities, the Orthodox Church does not afford the Bible the central importance that it has among Protestants. Moreover it insists that the Bible can only be fully understood within the context of the worshipping community which gives it its authority, authenticity and inspiration.

Asia and Australasia

The work of translating and printing the Bible in Asia and Australasia has been a massive undertaking, but considerable progress was made in the 20th century – not least in China and India.

Asia is a vast continent. The influence of the Bible has been patchy, largely associated with the missionary expansion which took place at the end of the 18th and beginning of the 19th centuries. The Bible often played a prominent part in this evangelization, as the early missionaries translated parts of it as the needs of the local people determined.

The work of Hudson Taylor in the late 19th century laid the foundations for missionary activity in China.

China

In 1807 Robert Morrison was the first Protestant missionary allowed into China and he was only allowed to stay because he was employed as a translator by the East India Company. In his free time he translated the Bible and wrote a dictionary. The legacy of his work was continued by Hudson Taylor who founded the China Inland Mission in 1865.

For a long time China was closed to all outside Christian influence and even today the 'official Church' is closely controlled by the government. For decades it was necessary to smuggle in copies of the Bible, but restrictions were lessened in the 1980s. Theological colleges again received members and Bibles with other forms of Christian literature could be printed, studied and disseminated. Meanwhile the work of translating and printing goes on. The Bible, or part of it, is now available in 58 Chinese languages or dialects.

India

In 1793 the Baptist missionary William Carey landed in India. Together with his assistants he translated the New Testament into Bengali. Within 30 years parts of the Bible had been translated into 37 languages. This work of translation continued through the 19th century and into the 20th. In such a predominantly Hindu culture it was inevitable that the Christians in India would maintain and adapt many customs and traditions from the surrounding culture. The work of translating, teaching and spreading the message of the Bible has to be understood against this backcloth. The Bible, or a portion of it, now exists in over 140 Indian languages and dialects.

Theology of compassion is the theology of love with no strings attached. It does not predetermine how and where God should do God's saving work. It does not assume that God left Asia in the hands of pagan powers and did not come to it until missionaries from the West reached it.

CHOAN-SENG SONG,
TAIWANESE THEOLOGIAN

Part of the congregation in a packed church in the Cook Islands.

THE BIBLE IN AUSTRALASIA

In 1818, the first book of the Bible to be published in any Pacific language was a Gospel for Tahiti. Today there are around 90 projects being undertaken in the Asia Pacific region by the United Bible Societies. The first Bible Society branch in Australia was formed in 1817 and in New Zealand in 1848. The most widely used versions in Australia today are the New International Version and the Good News Bible.

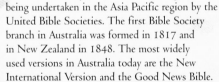

The Bible Society in Australia publishes Bibles in English as well as in Aboriginal and Torres Strait Island languages, and helps with the translation, editing and typesetting of biblical materials in both Australian and regional languages. The first complete Bible in an Aboriginal language will be the Kriol Bible, which is due for completion in 2003–2004.

Art

Art has provided an opportunity over the centuries for people to express their feelings about biblical subjects and the depth of their faith. While some have painted from a deep commitment to the Church, others have worked outside the Christian community.

Excavations from churches and synagogues dating from the third century CE onwards have shown that paintings of scenes from the Old and New Testaments were commonplace from an early time. Art was used in the catacombs in the third and fourth centuries both to illustrate and also interpret biblical stories. In particular, such stories as Noah and the ark and Daniel in the lion's den were used to anticipate the saving and healing ministry of Jesus.

The Middle Ages

During the 11th and 12th centuries the Romanesque style of art and architecture encouraged both narrative and symbolic representation of Christian themes. The incarnation, for instance, was seen as the summit of human culture with universal meaning for all time. Illuminated manuscripts and frescos were a feature of the time. During the Gothic period of the 13th and 15th centuries, art moved towards a greater realism, but many formerly popular themes, such as the birth, life and death of Jesus, are noticeably absent from this period.

The Renaissance

Renaissance artists painted and sculpted even more realistically, drawing on classical sculpture for their inspiration. This realism is apparent in Donatello's painting entitled *Resurrection*, in which an austere, slime-covered Jesus emerges from the tomb to remind us that his suffering and death were real. Michelangelo's large-

REMBRANDT VAN RIJN

Rembrandt (1606–69) worked against the backdrop of the Reformation. His paintings of Old and New Testament scenes were deeply felt; they expressed both his own personal story and that of the human race. In his later paintings of the crucifixion, Rembrandt, through his own trials, participated in the sufferings of Christ.

The Church was the major patron of the arts in medieval Europe. *The Fall of Man and Expulsion from the Garden of Eden* (1508–12) by Michelangelo Buonarroti (1475–1564), from the Sistine Chapel ceiling, Vatican, Rome.

scale depictions of creation and the last judgment in the Sistine Chapel are celebrations of the human body.

Modern art

The watercolours and etchings of William Blake from the 18th and 19th centuries, especially his engravings for the book of Job, are imbued with fascination and power. The 19th-century Pre-Raphaelites depicted biblical themes with authenticity and feeling in a highly realistic style. In the 20th century, Graham Sutherland (1903–80) maintained that no one could understand the crucifixion except in the light of Auschwitz. His painting of the crucifixion in Coventry Cathedral powerfully unites symbolism and realism. Georges Roualt (1871–1958) was heavily influenced by the iconic tradition in his portraits of Jesus, while his landscapes depict salvation and the presence of Christ. The work of Marc Chagall (1887–1985) in painting, etching and stained-glass windows suggests both the loneliness of suffering and the reassurance of hope.

> *Rembrandt experienced passion and pain, wealth and poverty, success and rejection. And he transformed these feelings into the strokes of his brush with such potency that few people can look at his paintings and remain unmoved. For part of their power is that they reach us where we are at, scratching around in the farmyard of life.*
>
> HELEN DE BORCHGRAVE,
> *A JOURNEY INTO CHRISTIAN ART*

Music

Ever since Old Testament times music has been used to enhance both Jewish and Christian worship and liturgy.

Although the Bible gives no indication of the melodies used in Jewish and early Christian worship, it contains a treasure-store of lyrics which were used after the time of the Jewish exile and by the early Christians.

Psalms and hymns

Over the centuries the Bible has been used in Western music to accompany and enhance Jewish and Christian worship through the congregational singing of psalms and hymns. The psalms in the Old Testament were written originally for communal singing both on special occasions, as during the Festival of Passover, and during normal Temple worship. Paul, in his letter to the Ephesians, tells us that the early Christians sang 'psalms and hymns and spiritual songs'.

The main Christian denominations have made extensive use of the Magnificat and the Benedictus in their worship. Much of the Roman Catholic Mass is taken directly from the Bible and this service proved irresistible to such composers as Mozart and Verdi, who have set it to some of their most sublime music.

Medieval liturgical music

The most important figure in medieval liturgical music was Pope Gregory I, who had chants collected and assigned to different liturgical occasions – the 'Gregorian Chant'. This music was the servant of faith,

A page from a book of anthems produced for Eton College, early 16th century.

Johann Sebastian Bach (1685–1750), whose Christian faith found its expression in his music. *Johann Sebastian Bach* (c. 1720) by Johann Jakob Ihle (1702–74).

since it did not interpret the text but set out to create the right atmosphere in which the heart and mind became amenable to religious faith and pious devotion.

Anthems, motets and oratorios

Around 1000 CE monophony (single-voice) was replaced by polyphony (multi-voice), allowing for a much more complex interpretation of biblical themes. This led to the growth of anthems and motets – complex musical forms designed to be sung by choirs

> *Whether the angels play only Bach praising God I am not sure. I am sure, however, that en famille they play Mozart.*
>
> KARL BARTH,
> SWISS PROTESTANT THEOLOGIAN

rather than congregations. Some of the most notable motets were written in the 19th century by Johannes Brahms, such as his setting of Psalm 51. Earlier, in the 18th century, J.S. Bach had written hundreds of cantatas, often to accompany selected readings from the lectionary. The oratorio is a more dramatic musical form that in time almost became a sacred opera: Handel's *Messiah* is the most popular of all religious oratorios and is largely an extended comment on verses from both the Old and New Testaments.

Biblical operas and secular music

By the 17th century various operas were written using biblical themes, most of them by Catholic composers such as Charpentier, who wrote *David et Jonathan* (1688). The 19th century saw many biblical operas – Rossini's *Moses in Egypt*, Guonod's *The Queen of Sheba* and Massenet's *Herodiade* among them. There has also been a wealth of secular biblical music, including Ralph Vaughan Williams' *Job: A Masque for Dancing* and Ernest Bloch's *Schelomo* (Solomon) for cello and orchestra.

Literature

The influence of the Bible and its worldview on modern literature has been immense and complex. It is in the influence of biblical allusion and motif rather than of actual borrowed language or narrative plot that the influence has been most keenly felt.

Over the centuries the Bible and its worldview have had an immense and complex impact on literature. Up until the modern era, all writers wrote against a backdrop of the generally accepted Christian view of the universe, but since the 19th century the Christian contribution to literature has been harder to identify – becoming more oblique and allusive. It is with modern literature that we deal here.

The empty heaven

The leading atheistic and nihilistic writers of the 20th century, such as Jean-Paul Sartre and Albert Camus, together with the dramatists of the Absurd, such as Beckett and Pirandello, conducted a lifelong argument with the worldview of the Bible waving their fists at what they took to be an empty heaven. Beckett's play *Waiting for Godot*, one of the most outstanding pieces of non-drama in the 20th century, is full of futile nostalgia for the world of the Bible with

Vladimir, one of the characters waiting for Godot, wondering why only one of the evangelists mentioned the repentant thief while also trying to remember a verse from Proverbs. Given the futility of Vladimir's existence the idea is amusing.

An alternative Jesus

Allusion apart, there have also been many attempts in modern

A scene from the play *Waiting for Godot*, Barbican Theatre, London, 1999.

> *Agony, then, is struggle. And Christ came to bring us agony, struggle and not peace. He told us as much. 'Do not think that I have come to bring peace on earth.'... Christ, our Christ! Why hast thou forsaken us?*
>
> MIGUEL DE UNAMONO

literature to present alternative understandings of the person of Jesus. In *The Last Temptation of Christ* Nikos Kazantzakis pictures Jesus as being tempted to exchange the cross for a life of simple pleasure. When this book was made into a film it was the suggested sexual liaison between Christ and Mary Magdalene that caused most offence to Christians. Offence of a different kind was given by Dorothy L. Sayers in her series of radio plays, *The Man Born to be King*, broadcast in 1943 during the throes of the Second World War. Sayers set her plays in first-century Palestine but had the characters speak in colloquial dialect. This shocked Christians still largely living in a world of the Authorized Version and hushed voices in church.

In the middle of the 20th century a series of novels emerged from North America which brought a largely apocalyptic tone to the immensely charged social and personal settings they described. Among them were John Steinbeck's *Grapes of Wrath* and *East of Eden*, James Baldwin's *Fire Next Time* and William Faulkner's *Go Down, Moses*. The biblical allusions which are such a large part of these novels were perhaps used to lend weight and gravitas to their apocalyptic tone.

Film

Over-familiarity is the main problem faced by anyone who wants to represent Jesus or depict a biblical event – such as the exodus of the Jews from Egypt or the giving of the Ten Commandments – on film. Films with biblical themes have also tended to be cloying and sentimental.

For centuries biblical themes and Jesus have been represented in paintings, sculptures and stained-glass windows with great frequency, and since the invention of moving pictures in the 1890s on the cinema screen as well. The earliest Jesus movie was *La Passion* (1897) followed by an American film about Jesus, *The Passion Play of Oberammergau*, which was actually shot, despite its title, on a rooftop in Manhattan. These early efforts to present Jesus met with strong opposition from the Church and local Christian groups who believed that they had a monopoly over everything to do with the figure who stood at the centre of Christianity – a belief underlined when *From the Manger to the Cross* was first shown in 1912.

Biblical epics

Moviemakers came to love biblical epics because they were popular with cinema-goers and they provided an opportunity

It is both bad taste and artistically ineffective to sandwich a picture about Jesus between a juggler's act and a Broadway song and dance.

FILM CRITIC OF *FROM THE MANGER TO THE CROSS*, 1912

for a story to be painted on a large canvas. Cecil B. De Mille's *King of Kings* (1927) was the first of the genre, but it also had the serious motive of setting out to exonerate Jews generally of all responsibility for the death of Jesus by pinning blame solely on the High Priest. This film was released just as the era of silent films was coming to an end.

Quo Vadis (1951) gave Jesus a bit part and concentrated on the martyrdom of Peter and the early Christians. The film ushered in the golden age of the biblical epic. In Nicholas Ray's *King of Kings* (1961) Jesus had no sense of his personal mission, while *Ben Hur* was far more memorable for its chariot race than anything of spiritual significance.

In the 1970s two films about Jesus developed out of stage plays and asked questions in keeping with the times. In *Jesus Christ Superstar* (1973) Pilate reflected the postmodern spirit of the time when he not only asked, 'What is truth?' but went on to say, 'We both have truths. Are mine the same as yours?' In *Godspell* the anti-institutionalism of the period is reflected in the portrayal of Jesus as a clown; in *Gospel Road*, made around the same time in the 1970s, he was a juggler.

One last, but very interesting, example. Monty Python's *Life of Brian* (1979) was a clever send-up of biblical epics and first-century Palestinian politics. With its four-letter words and single episode of full-frontal nudity the film was bound to raise Christian hackles – and it did. However, the film did not mock Jesus but the sort of crowds which went looking for messiahs all over Palestine. The title refers to a Palestinian revolutionary who is mistaken for a prophet.

A scene from *King of Kings*, Cecil B. De Mille's 1927 interpretation of the life of Jesus.

The Qur'an and the Bible

The Jewish scriptures, the Christian Bible and the Muslim Qur'an have very close links. Muslims look upon the followers of each religion as 'People of the Book'.

The sacred book of the Muslims, the Qur'an, repeatedly claims that a direct line of revelation runs between it and the holy books of the Jews and the Christians (the Judaic-Christian tradition). It acknowledges these two religions to be, along with itself, 'Religions of the Book', since the holy books of all three were given to the holy prophets by Allah (God). These holy books are frequently acknowledged in the Qur'an – especially the *Tawrat* (Torah), the *Zabur* (Psalms) and the *Injil* (Gospel). Jews and Christians are encouraged to live by the light which their own holy books shed on the spiritual path.

The Qur'an

Although Muslims believe that the Qur'an and the Bible were both revealed by Allah they present markedly different ways of understanding key religious figures and events. The Qur'an, according to its own witness, offers a fuller and more complete understanding of the mind of Allah. As far as the

teachings of the Mosaic Law are concerned, the Qur'an makes it clear that some of its provisions were made because of the people's rebellion; they are thus incomplete or superseded by a superior revelation. Jesus relaxed some of these provisions and the Prophet of Allah (Muhammad) relaxed them still more. For

A Saudi Arabian boy reading the Qur'an.

> *We believe in Allah and that which was sent down to us, in Abraham, Ishmael, Isaac, Jacob and the Tribes of Israel and that which was given to Moses and to Jesus and that which was given to all the Prophets from their Lord. We make no difference between any of them for it is to Allah that we have submitted.*
>
> QUR'AN 2:136

study of each other's scriptures has been taking place for some time. As a result many Christians have come to see the close affinity between their scriptures and the Qur'an in many areas. At the same time Muslims have come to understand many of the Judaic-Christian scriptures to which their own Qur'an makes frequent reference. Both have come to appreciate the large measure of overlap which exists between their holy books. Mutual understanding of this can only lead to an increased tolerance between them in the future.

Muslims, the Qur'an reveals Muhammad as the final and definitive revelation by which all other divine revelations must be judged. When revelations conflict then the Qur'an is seen as the final arbiter.

Dialogue
Dialogue between Muslims and Christians based on a patient

TAHRIF

Islam has also sought to deal with the discrepancies between the Qur'an and other scriptures by the notion of *tahrif*. This alleges that the older People of the Book have changed or corrupted their holy books in such a way that their teachings no longer agree with the Qur'an. On more than one occasion in the Qur'an they are charged with altering their holy books to suit

their own purposes. It is not quite certain, however, whether the charge is one of deliberately corrupting (changing) the text itself or simply changing its meaning. The final charge against Jews and Christians, however, is that they have misused their holy books.

The Bible and Judaism

By the time that the second Temple in Jerusalem had been built, scripture had taken its place at the heart of Jewish religious life. The later rabbinical additions, known as the Oral Torah, were given considerable authority through to the present time.

Judaism is very much a 'Religion of the Book' today, but this was not always the case. Before the Jews were taken into Babylonian exile in 586 BCE their faith was centred around the human life-cycle (birth, marriage and death) and the main events in the

Scripture at the heart
Between the time that the second Temple was built in Jerusalem (538 BCE) and the destruction of Herod's Temple (70 CE) a general consensus appeared about the canon of scripture, with certain books being given great spiritual

Solomon dictates the Proverbs. From the *Bible Historiale*, 1357.

agricultural year. Occasionally prophets appeared among the people to communicate God's word, while special visits to the Temple in Jerusalem gave the priests there the opportunity to pass on their teachings, mainly about the Torah, to the people.

authority within the community. By 70 CE the Pentateuch, the Prophets and the Writings, including some of the Psalms, were in place as the foundation of the canon.

A very important factor in all this was the growing feeling that God was no longer speaking directly to the people through his messengers, the prophets. The will of God for the people had already been revealed, especially through the Law and the Prophets, and all the principles were in place for the people to live lives that were pleasing to God. As people began to study the written Torah in the schools attached to their synagogues, so the regular festivals began to take on a greater religious significance and their agricultural significance diminished. They were linked to great events in Israel's past, such as the creation of the world, the institution of the Sabbath day, the exodus from Egypt and the giving of the Law on Mount Sinai. The scriptural accounts of these events were read as part of the festival celebrations.

Commentaries on the scriptures

In the years following the destruction of Jerusalem the most important development was the growth of rabbinic Judaism, a movement which has dominated Judaism to the present time. The first document to emerge from this movement was the Mishnah,

> *Turn Torah over and over again for everything is in it. Grow old and worn in it, and do not stir from it, for you have no better rule than it.*
>
> THE MISHNAH

produced around 200 CE. This codified the Jewish law as regards agriculture, the place of women, the payment of damages and the treatment of holy things. The Mishnah was studied later and two Talmuds (commentaries on the Mishnah) from Palestine and Babylon were produced. Incorporated into the Mishnah and the two Talmuds was the teaching of all the great Jewish sages from the second to the sixth centuries on a wide collection of topics. A series of commentaries on the whole of the Pentateuch, the Five Scrolls (Ruth, Esther, Song of Songs, Lamentations and Ecclesiastes), together with much of the remainder of the Hebrew Bible – called *Midrashim* – were made.

Although the rabbinic works did not quite possess the authority of scripture, especially the Torah, they came to have a considerable effect on the Jewish community. Even today matters of dispute and debate within the community are settled, if possible, by reference to the teaching of this vast body of ancient documents.

Feminism

Since the 1960s there has been fierce debate over whether the Bible has been a major cause of women's subjection and whether this subordination is maintained by the structures still to be found in Jewish and Christian societies.

There has been a great change throughout much of the Western world in the status and role of women in recent decades. Better education and training have enhanced opportunities in the workplace. This has led many to challenge the perceived teaching of the Bible on the place of women – not least because virtually all biblical scholarship for almost two centuries has been in the hands of men.

The feminist thesis

In 1837 Sarah Grimke suggested that biblical interpretation was deliberately biased against women to keep them in subjection. This was supported in 1895 by the publication of *The Women's Bible*, a series of essays which challenged the idea that the cultural, moral and religious norms of the Bible could be applied unquestioningly to modern life. Debate on the subject was only seriously opened up during the struggle for women's rights which took place in the 1960s. Critical attention concentrated on the status and role of women within the Christian and Jewish religious traditions and the part played by the Bible in maintaining the unfair status quo.

This enquiry into the Bible's role has centred on five main areas:

◆ The need to find out more about the status and role of women in biblical cultures. We still know very little.
◆ The quest for a more complete and balanced picture of the actual teaching of the Bible on issues relating to gender.

> *Women whose lives have been shaped by feminism can no longer continue to read ancient scriptural texts and patriarchal traditions in old, established ways.*
>
> NICOLA SLEE, BRITISH FEMINIST THEOLOGIAN AND WRITER

◆ The growth of alternative interpretations of biblical texts to show that they do not necessarily present a negative view of the role of women. Phyllis Trible and Elizabeth Schussler Fiorenza, for instance, have both argued that Paul's insistence on women keeping silent in Christian worship was in response to a

◆ To make fresh translations of the Bible which seek to reduce the amount of gender-exclusive language in the text.

Some feminists conclude that the Bible is irredeemably sexist. Their experiences both inside and outside the Church, together with their perception of the Bible as patriarchal in

Women leading a service in a church in Guatemala.

particular local problem and was never intended to be an instrument for the general subjugation of women.
◆ To develop a more complete picture of God in the Bible by applying feminine images, such as that of a woman and mother, to the deity. Ultimately, however, God is beyond all masculine and feminine categories, even though such categories can be spiritually useful.

essence, rules out any commitment on their part to the Jewish or Christian communities. Many women continue to regard the Bible as authoritative and remain active within their church or synagogue. At times, though, the tight-rope they walk is an uncomfortable one.

Postmodernism

Postmodernism is one of the most important philosophical movements of the 20th and 21st centuries and, as such, is having a tremendous effect on the way that people look at religion in general and the Bible in particular.

Some see the avant-garde culture of the 1920s as the early stirrings of postmodernism, while Arnold Toynbee, who was one of the first to use the term, looked further back to the crisis of modernity in the 19th century, which erupted into the open after the First World War.

Modernity and grand narratives

'Modernity' refers to trends in philosophy, politics and culture since the Enlightenment of the 18th century. Modernists believed in the idea of progress and a great deal of philosophy and religion shared this optimism; science, Marxism and Christianity all attempted to explain everything and promised solutions to the world's problems. Thus, the idea of 'progress' was linked to what postmodernists call 'grand narratives': overarching belief systems which claim universal legitimacy and authority. For various reasons, such as the atom bomb, ecological crisis and the demise of state Marxism, these grand narratives have collapsed.

At the same time, globalization has led to a proliferation of 'signs' – the messages and symbols with which the media bombard us every day. These signs have lost what little context they once had; we can pick and choose our lifestyles and our religions; when we grow tired of one, we can choose another. Images such as the cross of Christianity are 'free-floating', meaning

The crucifix, at one time a powerful reminder of the sacrificial death of Christ, is for many people today just another item of jewellery. Those who wear it may be quite unaware of its significance.

> *Modernism tore up unity and postmodernism has been enjoying the shreds.*
>
> TODD GITLIN,
> NORTH AMERICAN WRITER

they are often little more than accessories or jewellery; they do not refer back to anything of significance. Similarly, the Bible is just one book among many, whose claim to universal truth is no longer a factor in a relativized world. This is the condition in which postmodernists claim the world finds itself: not an irreligious world as much as a world of competing religious symbols and styles of living, none of which can claim our allegiance for long.

Postmodernism finds itself at home in the literature produced by French thinkers such as Emmanuel Levinas and Jacques Derrida. It also expresses itself noticeably in the world of modern architecture – in the artificial and superficial world of commercial transaction, shopping precincts, supermarkets and concrete. The superficiality of postmodernism is a caustic comment on the dreams and hopes of secular humanism and liberalism.

Postmodernism and the Bible

As far as a postmodern approach to the Bible is concerned three principles should be borne in mind:

◆ the importance of language in the making of our worlds.
◆ the cultural and ideological background of the Bible, both of which obscure its truth for modern people.
◆ a healthy distrust must be shown towards any grand narratives – theories which are intended to explain the whole of reality.

The Bible in an Electronic Age

The electronic media are beginning to have a considerable effect on biblical studies and this is certain to become more important and influential in the future.

The modern study of the texts of the Bible is being transformed by the revolution brought about by the microchip. In particular, the electronic media are extremely useful for organizing, storing and publishing information about biblical texts. Linguistic databases and reference tools are now available for the task of unravelling many of the remaining mysteries of the text of the Bible.

Work on the text

Computer programmes can now help scholars to reconstruct whole texts from fragments of manuscript evidence, in much the same way as ceramic vessels, for instance, can be built up from small shards of material. These programmes can also go further and suggest links between different manuscripts, so allowing scholars to recognize 'family' resemblances among ancient manuscripts – a very necessary intermediate stage in reaching a full understanding of the text.

Editing the texts

Holding text in electronic form is immediately useful since it allows editing, querying, recording and displaying to take place. In this way words, clauses, sentences, paragraphs and other literary forms can be analysed and examined. Already, a considerable body of information has been built up about the Jewish scriptures, the Septuagint and the New Testament.

Constructing a concordance

Concordances are one of the most important aids to serious Bible study. Traditionally, such concordances have been in book form and simply trace a single word through the biblical texts. Perhaps the most important asset that computers have brought to a study of the Bible is the construction of a dynamic concordance of the biblical text. Computer

Even in remote parts of the world, the computer is proving to be a useful tool for students of the Bible. An Orthodox priest in Kazakhstan.

programmes are able to search for much more subtle nuances, such as the use of grammatical devices in an individual book which the author has used to create a particular kind of effect.

At the moment computer software programmes developed for use with the humanities are available, but biblical scholars have been slow to grasp their significance and make use of this new tool. As these programmes become more sophisticated, however, the computer is bound to have a much more profound effect on our understanding of the Bible. Trends towards providing compact mass storage, with a single disk now capable of holding upwards of 150 books, and smaller, more powerful, microcomputers can only ensure the increasing use of the computer in religious studies.

Rapid Factfinder

A

Aaron: Moses' older brother; Israel's first High Priest; assisted Moses in asking the Pharaoh to release the Israelites.

Abraham: main recipient of God's promises to the Jewish nation in the Old Testament; first of Israel's patriarchal figures.

Acts of the Apostles: fifth book in the New Testament; continues the story from where the Gospels left off; describes the birth and early witness of the Church; dominated by Peter and then Paul.

Ahab: king of Israel from around 874 to 852 BCE; married to Jezebel, who wanted to introduce worship of the pagan deity Baal to Israel; had a running battle with Elijah the prophet.

Allah: God in Islam.

Amos: prophet active in Israel around 760 BCE; unpopular because he prophesied the downfall of the kingdom unless it repented.

Antioch: Syrian city; location of the first major Christian church which sent Paul on his missionary journeys.

Apocrypha: collection of books of secondary importance included in Roman Catholic and Orthodox Bibles; sometimes, but not always, included between the Old and New Testaments of Protestant Bibles.

apostle: 'one who is sent'; name given to Jesus' disciples after the Day of Pentecost, as they were sent into the world to bear witness to the message of Jesus and to continue his work.

Aramaic: language closely related to Hebrew; widely spoken from the eighth century BCE to the New Testament period; everyday language of Jesus and his disciples.

Ark of the Covenant: golden box placed between two cherubim in the Holy of Holies in the Tabernacle and the Temple; contained the Ten Commandments, a jar of manna and Aaron's rod that budded.

Assyria: country in what is now known as northern Iraq; established the most powerful empire in the Middle East during the eighth and seventh centuries BCE.

Authorized Version: English translation of the Bible published in 1611; adopted later for public reading in church; also known as the King James Version.

B

Baal: main god of the Canaanites; a god of nature and of war; proven powerless in a contest with Yahweh initiated by the prophet Elijah on Mount Carmel.

Babylon: city on the River Euphrates in what is now Iraq; centre of one of the world's greatest early empires.

baptism: dipping or immersing in water; originally a Jewish practice; adopted by the early Church as an initiation ceremony.

Barnabas: Jewish-Cypriot leader in the early Church; had an important ministry of encouragement; accompanied Paul on an early missionary journey but later parted from him.

base communities: groups of laypeople in Central and South American countries who meet to study their own situation in the light of the Bible.

Benedictus: Latin name for the prophecy of Zechariah, the father of John the Baptist, celebrating his son's birth; used in public worship in both Roman Catholic and Anglican churches.

Benjamin: youngest son of Jacob; kept at home while his half-brothers went to Egypt in search of food; agent of his half-brothers' reconciliation with his full brother Joseph.

Bethlehem: village nine kilometres south of Jerusalem; home of King David and birthplace of Jesus in fulfilment of Micah's prophecy.

Bible: 'books'; Christian scriptures consisting of the Old and New Testaments and containing 66 books; Jewish scriptures consisting of 39 books.

Book of Common Prayer: major prayer book of the Anglican Church; first appeared in 1549 and established in 1662; largely the work of Archbishop Cranmer.

C

John Calvin: Swiss Protestant Reformer, theologian and church founder; lived from 1509 to 1564; leader of the Reformation in Geneva.

Canaan: Jewish Promised Land; later called Israel.

canon: 'measure'; choice of books to be included in the scriptures; standard against which behaviour and belief can be tested.

catholic epistles: James, 1 and 2 Peter, 1, 2 and 3 John and Jude; with the exception of 2 and 3 John, these New Testament letters addressed a more general audience than a local church or person; also known as the universal epistles.

1 and 2 Chronicles: included in the Writings of the Hebrew scriptures; trace the story of Israel from Adam to the return of the Jewish exiles from Babylon.

Circumcision: removal of the foreskin of the penis on the eighth day after birth; oldest Jewish ritual still practised today.

Colossians: New Testament letter; probably written by Paul from prison in either 60 or 61 CE; deals with false teaching – the so-called 'Colossian heresy'.

Communion: central act of Christian worship involving the eating of bread and the drinking of wine to commemorate the death of Jesus.

1 and 2 Corinthians: Paul's letters to the church he founded at Corinth; contain key teachings on love, and about the Church as the body of Christ.

Council of Carthage: Church Council of 390 CE at which the canon of the New Testament was formally settled.

Court of Israel: third courtyard in Herod's Temple, open only to male Jews.

Court of Priests: innermost courtyard in Herod's Temple, exclusively for priests, except during the Festival of Tabernacles, when Jewish men were allowed to walk around the altar.

Court of the Gentiles: outer courtyard in Herod's Temple, open to both Jews and Gentiles.

Court of Women: second courtyard in Herod's Temple, open to both male and female Jews.

Cyrus the Great: Persian emperor from 539 to 530 BCE; conquered Babylon and encouraged the Jewish exiles to return home.

D

Daniel: Old Testament book concerning the faith of Daniel

and his friends; the second half describes Daniel's visions.

David: Israel's second and greatest king who ruled from 1010 to 970 BCE; received God's promise that his dynasty would be an eternal one; gifted musician and writer of many psalms.

Day of Atonement: most serious day in the Jewish year, during which people seek God's forgiveness through repentance, prayer and fasting; lasts for 25 hours; also called Yom Kippur.

Day of Pentecost: day on which the Holy Spirit was given to the Church, as recorded in the Acts of the Apostles; celebrated as the birthday of the Christian Church.

Dead Sea: Palestine's largest inland body of water, into which the River Jordan flows; inhospitable land 366 metres below sea level.

Dead Sea Scrolls: collection of 500 manuscripts discovered on the shores of the Dead Sea in 1947; one of the most important biblical archaeological discoveries of the 20th century.

Deborah: prophetess and one of Israel's judges; the song of Deborah is thought to be one of the oldest-known pieces of Hebrew poetry.

Decalogue: 'ten words'; the Ten Commandments, or Ten Sayings.

Delilah: Philistine woman who betrayed Samson to the Philistines by persuading him to tell her the secret of his strength.

Deuteronomist: one of four original sources for the Pentateuch; found almost exclusively in the book of Deuteronomy; referred to as the symbol 'D' in Old Testament source criticism.

Deuteronomy: one of the five books in the Pentateuch; provides a summary of the whole Law found elsewhere in the Torah.

Diaspora: 'dispersion'; the scattering of Jews across the ancient world as a result of their exile by the Babylonians.

E

Ecclesiastes: book of wise sayings about the meaninglessness of life without God; part of the Writings in the Jewish scriptures.

Ehud: left-handed judge who assassinated Eglon, a Moabite king.

Elijah: prophet active in the northern kingdom of Israel during the ninth century BCE; fierce opponent of corrupt kings and the importing of pagan practices into Israel.

Elisha: Elijah's successor as prophet of Israel.

Elohist: one of four original sources for the Pentateuch; in this source the word 'Elohim' is used for the divine name; thought to come from the ninth or eighth centuries BCE; referred to by the symbol 'E' in Old Testament source criticism.

Ephesians: letter written by Paul to Christians in the Greek city of Ephesus; focuses on the new, joyous life available through Christ.

Epic of Gilgamesh: masterpiece of Near-Eastern literature famous for its description of a universal flood that is much earlier than the Genesis account.

epistle: any of the letters in the New Testament, written by Paul, Peter, John and others.

Essenes: group within Palestinian Judaism that existed from the second century BCE to 70 CE;

formed a community at Qumran, which produced the Dead Sea Scrolls.

Esther: Jewish woman who became the queen of the Persian king Xerxes and whose faith was crucial in enabling the Jews in Persia to escape a plot to eliminate them; book included in the Writings of the Jewish scriptures.

Eucharist: 'thanksgiving'; name given by some Churches to the central act of Christian worship, Holy Communion.

exodus: journey of the Jews out of Egyptian slavery to freedom in the Promised Land.

Exodus: book in the Pentateuch describing the escape of the Jews, under the leadership of Moses, from slavery in Egypt.

Ezekiel: priest who prophesied to the Babylonian exiles; his name is given to a book in the Old Testament containing the reassuring message that God is with his people even in exile.

Ezra: key reformer in post-exilic Judaism who established the Law of God in a community that had returned to Jerusalem after exile in Babylonia.

F

form criticism: type of biblical criticism applied to both Old and New Testaments that sought to discover how material had been shaped during the earliest period of Church life, when it was circulated by word of mouth.

Former Prophets: subdivision of the Prophets in the Hebrew scriptures comprising the books of Joshua, Judges, 1 and 2 Samuel and 1 and 2 Kings, which are attributed to the early prophets Joshua, Samuel and Jeremiah; treated as works of prophetic

literature by Hebrew tradition but regarded as historical in Christian tradition.

G

Galatians: epistle of Paul to the Christians in Galatia in response to false teaching; may have been written as early as 48 CE.

Galilee: upland area of northern Palestine where Jesus grew up; Jesus spent most of his ministry in Lower Galilee.

Genesis: 'beginnings'; first book of the Bible; tells the story of the creation of the world, the birth of the Jewish nation under Abraham and the descent into Egyptian slavery.

Gentile: a non-Jew.

Gideon: one of the judges; led Israel for 40 years; turned down the offer of kingship; compromised with pagan idols.

Good News Bible: highly successful translation of the Bible first published in the 1970s.

gospel: 'good news' about the resurrection of Christ that Christians are committed to sharing with others.

Gospel: 'good news'; name given by the early Christian Church to each of the four books in the New Testament that tells the story of Jesus.

H

Habakkuk: Old Testament prophet in Jerusalem who taught that God was using the Babylonians to punish Israel.

Haggai: prophet in the sixth century BCE; concerned that the Temple in Jerusalem should be rebuilt after the return from exile.

Hanukkah: Jewish festival celebrating the cleansing of the

Temple in the second century BCE by Judas Maccabeus after it had been defiled by Antiochus IV Epiphanes.

Hebrew: main language of the Old Testament; spoken in Israel for much of the Old Testament period; replaced by Aramaic for everyday use after the exile.

Hebrews: anonymous but extensive New Testament letter written to Jewish Christians, probably in the seventh decade CE.

Herod the Great: ruler of Palestine from 37 to 4 BCE; tried to kill the infant Jesus; built the third Temple in Jerusalem.

Hezekiah: king of Judah from 715 to 687 BCE; a good king who saved the country from being incorporated into the Assyrian empire.

High Priest: leader of the Jewish community; Caiaphas was High Priest from 18 to 36 CE and was present at Jesus' trial.

Holy of Holies: area at the heart of the Temple in Jerusalem; the dwelling-place of God; only entered by the High Priest once a year.

Holy Spirit: third member of the Christian Trinity.

Hosea: prophet from the northern kingdom of Israel in the eighth century BCE; used his own domestic experiences to highlight the faithlessness of Israel.

I

icon: stylized painting of Jesus, the holy family or a saint used as a devotional aid by Orthodox Christians.

Isaac: the promised son of Abraham and Sarah.

Isaiah: prophet who lived in Jerusalem in the eighth century BCE; the Old Testament book earing his name probably includes rophecies from two or three rophets, and is perhaps best nown for prophecies looking orward to the coming of the Messiah.

srael: nation which inherited the ovenant promises that God first nade to Abraham; name of the and of Canaan given to this ation as their promised home.

acob: one of the three patriarchs; randson of Abraham; ancestor of he 12 tribes of Israel through his 2 sons.

ames: brother of Jesus; one of he leaders in the early Jerusalem Church; writer of the earliest pistle in the New Testament.

ephthah: one of the judges; ed the Israelites against the Ammonites; sacrificed his daughter after making a careless vow to God.

eremiah: major Old Testament prophet who was active in the southern kingdom of Judah from 626 to 587 BCE; sometimes known as the 'weeping prophet' because of his predictions of catastrophe, although he also had a message of hope; finally taken unwillingly to Egypt by the Jewish exiles.

Jericho: ancient city just north of the Dead Sea whose origins go back to 8000 BCE; its walls famously collapsed as the result of an attack by Joshua.

Jeroboam I and Jeroboam II: Jeroboams I and II were both kings of Israel and both were highly criticized by the prophets of their day; under Jeroboam II Israel had one of its most successful periods.

Jerome: ascetic who lived from around 341 to 420 CE; his Latin

translation of the Bible is known as the Vulgate.

Jerusalem: city captured by David from the Jebusites which became the capital of the united Israel; location of the Temple.

Jerusalem Bible: official Bible of the Roman Catholic Church; published in 1966.

Job: lead character in the Old Testament book of Job whose experiences of hardship and rejection form the basis of a profound treatise on suffering.

Joel: Old Testament prophet who prophesied in Jerusalem in the fifth century BCE; his message was for the Jews who had returned from exile in Babylon and was concerned with the 'Day of the Lord'.

John: disciple of Jesus; part of the inner circle of Jesus' disciples along with Peter and James; nicknamed 'Boanerges' ('Son of Thunder'); may or may not have written the Gospel that is named after him.

1, 2 and 3 John: New Testament epistles written by the author of John's Gospel; all three were probably composed in the last decade of the first century CE; in them the author denounces false teaching and reassures his readers.

John the Baptist: son of Zechariah and Elizabeth; cousin and eventual baptizer of Jesus; appears in all four Gospels as the forerunner of Jesus; killed by Herod the Great.

Jonah: seventh-century BCE prophet who disobeyed God and was swallowed by a large fish; preached judgment against Nineveh instead of God's message of love.

Joshua: one of the Former Prophets; took over leadership of the Israelites when Moses died on

the verge of the Promised Land and led them into Canaan.

Josiah: king of Judah from 640 to 609 BCE; began a religious reformation leading to the discovery of the scroll of the Law; killed tragically.

Judah: most important of the 12 tribes of Israel.

Judas Maccabeus: succeeded his father, Mattathias, in fighting the Syrians; purified the Temple after his victories; his story is told in the Apocrypha; killed in 160 BCE.

Jude: brother of Jesus; may have written the short New Testament letter that bears his name and shares almost all of its material with 2 Peter.

Judges: 12 tribal leaders who led groups of Israelites during the early days of occupation of the Promised Land; book in the Old Testament.

K

kingdom of God: idea at the heart of Jesus' teaching; Jesus called people to accept the kingship of God in the spiritual kingdom on earth that he was building.

1 and 2 Kings: books telling the story of the reigns of the kings, starting with Solomon and then following the divided kingdoms of Israel in the north and Judah in the south, until the fall of Israel in 722 BCE and then the fall of Jerusalem in 587 BCE; part of the Former Prophets.

kosher: 'fit'; food which is in keeping with the Jewish dietary laws laid down in the Torah and so is fit to be eaten.

L

L: symbol used to denote the source of material unique to Luke's Gospel.

Lamentations: five poems of lament written in response to the destruction of Jerusalem by the Babylonian army in 587 BCE; the first four poems are acrostics, in which each line begins with a different letter of the Hebrew alphabet.

Latter Prophets: the books of Isaiah, Jeremiah and Ezekiel (the Major Prophets) together with the books of the 12 Minor Prophets, from Hosea to Malachi; Christian tradition also includes the book of Daniel.

Leviticus: third book of the Torah; gives instructions for carrying out sacrifices and other ceremonies in ancient Israel.

liberation theology: approach to the Bible of many Christians, particularly in Central and South America, in which a preferential option for the poor is seen in the Gospels.

Lord's Prayer: prayer that Jesus taught his disciples; included within Jesus' Sermon on the Mount; the only prayer used universally by the Christian Church.

Lord's Supper: term used in some Protestant churches for Holy Communion.

Luke: doctor who was a close friend of Paul; accompanied Paul on some missionary journeys; author of the Gospel bearing his name and the Acts of the Apostles.

M

M: symbol used to denote the source of material unique to Matthew's Gospel.

Magnificat: Mary's song of praise in Luke's Gospel; sung in some Anglican and Orthodox services.

Major Prophets: Christian designation for the Old Testament

prophetic books of Isaiah, Jeremiah and Ezekiel.

Malachi: 'my messenger'; last but not latest book in the Old Testament; probably comes from the early fifth century BCE.

Mark: companion of Paul and Barnabas on an early missionary journey; his link with the Gospel bearing his name is tenuous since the tradition that he wrote it only began in the early second century.

Masoretes: rabbis who added vowel markings to the consonantal Hebrew text of the Old Testament between 500 and 1000 CE.

Matthew: one of Jesus' disciples; called to follow Jesus while collecting taxes; also called Levi; may have written the Gospel carrying his name.

Messiah: 'anointed one'; equivalent to the Greek word 'Christ'; describes the long-awaited deliverer who would establish God's kingdom and destroy Israel's enemies; believed by Christians to be Jesus.

Micah: eighth-century BCE prophet in Judah; younger contemporary of Isaiah.

Minor Prophets: 12 prophetic books at the end of the Old Testament, so-called because of the brevity of their prophecies.

Mishnah: supplementary laws given by God to Moses on Mount Sinai and handed down by word of mouth for centuries; part of the Talmud.

Moses: leader of the Israelites; chosen by God to lead the Israelites out of Egyptian slavery to the Promised Land; received the Ten Commandments on Mount Sinai; died within sight of Canaan.

Muhammad: 'the Prophet'; recipient of special revelations

from Allah which form the basis of the Qur'an.

Muratorian Fragment: incomplete Latin manuscript from around 190 CE listing certain New Testament books and giving an intriguing insight into which books were included in, or excluded from, the New Testament canon at that time; discovered in 1740 in Milan.

N

Nahum: Old Testament prophet who predicted the end of the Assyrian empire, especially the downfall of its capital city, Nineveh.

Nehemiah: appointed by the Persian king Artaxerxes I as governor over the returning Jewish exiles in Jerusalem in the fifth century BCE; was granted permission to rebuild the walls of Jerusalem; may have worked with Ezra to re-establish God's Law in the community.

Nero: Roman emperor from 54 to 68 CE; brutal ruler who blamed Christians for a serious fire in Rome and executed many; probably martyred Peter and Paul.

New English Bible: major English translation of the Bible; the New Testament was published first, in 1961, then the whole Bible was published in 1970; a revised edition (the Revised English Bible) was brought out in 1989.

New International Version: completely new translation of the Bible begun in 1965 and eventually published in its entirety in 1978; made with wide Evangelical support and input.

New Testament: second part of the Christian Bible; comprises 27 books: four Gospels, the Acts of the Apostles, a number of epistles, mainly written by Paul, and the book of Revelation.

New Year: Jewish festival at the end of the summer; marked by the blowing of the shofar in the synagogue; allows Jews the chance to make a fresh start in their lives; also called Rosh Hashanah.

Nineveh: capital city of Assyria; situated on the River Tigris in what is now northern Iraq; conquered by the Babylonians in 612 BCE.

Noah: saved with his family from the flood by building a large boat called the ark; God made a covenant with him to repopulate the earth after the waters receded.

Numbers: fourth book in the Pentateuch; describes Israel's travels through the wilderness from Mount Sinai to the verge of the Promised Land.

O

Obadiah: 'servant or worshipper of the Lord'; shortest book in the Old Testament; usually dated soon after the beginning of the exile in 587 BCE.

Old Testament: first part of the Christian Bible; comprises 39 books which are the same as those in the Jewish scriptures but in a different order.

P

Palestine: land that traditionally ran between the town of Dan in the north and Beersheba in the south; also known as Israel.

parable: story told by Jesus, taken from everyday life, intended to carry a moral or spiritual meaning.

Passover: annual Jewish pilgrimage festival celebrating the release of the Jewish slaves from Egypt; by the time of Jesus, Jews were coming from all over the Roman empire to celebrate Passover in the Jerusalem Temple; still celebrated by Jews today; also known as the Festival of Unleavened Bread or Pesach.

pastoral epistles: collective name for the New Testament letters of 1 and 2 Timothy and Titus, which deal with pastoral issues within the Church.

patriarchs: 'father figures'; Abraham, Isaac and Jacob, the three early Israelite leaders who laid the foundations of the nation.

Paul: outstanding leader of the early Church; tireless missionary responsible for founding many churches; author of many letters laying out the basics of the Christian faith which are included in the New Testament.

Pentateuch: 'five scrolls'; first five books of the Old Testament; also known by Jews as the Torah or the Law.

Pentecost: one of three major Jewish pilgrimage festivals; celebrated 50 days after Passover; marked the end of the grain harvest; also known as the Feast of Weeks or Shavuot.

Peter: leading disciple of Jesus; member of the inner circle of disciples; denied knowing Jesus before the cucifixion; leader of the early Church after the Day of Pentecost.

1 and 2 Peter: letters sent to Christians scattered throughout Asia Minor; 1 Peter warns of persecution and encourages faith in Jesus; 2 Peter warns against false teaching; the apostle Peter may have written the first letter, but it is unlikely that he wrote the second.

Pharisees: Jewish group that emerged in the second century BCE; emphasized strict observance of the Jewish law; opposed Jesus and were instrumental in bringing about his death.

Philemon: shortest and most personal of Paul's letters; written

to a leader in the church at Colosse about his runaway slave; urged conciliation and compassion.

Philippians: letter that Paul wrote from prison, probably in the early 60s CE; shows the warm relationship that existed between the writer and the recipients.

Philistines: group who moved into a coastal strip in Palestine in the 12th century BCE; became Israel's most powerful early enemy.

Pontius Pilate: Roman procurator of Palestine between 26 and 36 CE; known for his brutality; responsible for giving permission for the execution of Jesus.

postmodernism: movement in such diverse areas as literature, art and architecture that reacts against modern tendencies, often by harking back to previous conventions.

Priestly: one of four original sources for the Pentateuch; this source is almost exclusively concerned with the liturgy, priesthood and worship; referred to by the symbol 'P' in Old Testament source criticism.

prison epistles: Ephesians, Philippians, Colossians and Philemon – four letters that Paul probably wrote while in prison.

Promised Land: name by which the land of Canaan was known to the Israelites long before they settled there.

prophet: man or woman who senses a call from God to speak the divine word both about the present and the future.

Prophets: second division of the Jewish scriptures, comprising the books of the Former Prophets and the Latter Prophets.

Proverbs: book from the Writings section of the Jewish scriptures containing several collections of wise sayings – God's truth for everyday living.

Psalms: 'praises'; contains 150 hymns and prayers, some of which were composed by King David; longest book in the Bible.

Purim: Jewish festival celebrating the success of Esther in saving many Jews from massacre.

Q

Q: symbol denoting the source of about 230 verses found in Matthew's and Luke's Gospels, but not included in Mark; from the German word *Quelle*, meaning 'source'.

Qumran: village close to the Dead Sea where the Dead Sea Scrolls were found in 1947.

Qur'an: Muslim holy book.

R

rabbi: Jewish title for a religious teacher; often applied to Jesus.

Reformation: movement in the Western Christian Church in the 16th century which argued that the Bible and not the Church should be the sole ground of spiritual authority; led to the formation of many Protestant Churches.

Rehoboam: king of Judah from 930 to 908 BCE; son of King Solomon; northern and southern kingdoms separated during his reign.

Renaissance: 'new birth'; revival of art and literature from the 14th to the 16th centuries based on classical ideals; marked the transition from the Middle Ages to the modern world.

Revelation: last book of the Bible; contains the visions of Christ's supremacy that a man named John saw while imprisoned on the island of Patmos.

Revised Standard Version: revision of the American Standard Version, published in 1901, which was a revision of the Authorized Version of 1611; the New Testament was published in 1946 and the entire Bible in 1952; a revised edition (the New Revised Standard Version) was brought out in 1989.

Revised Version: translation of the Bible that attempted to update the Authorized Version; published in 1881.

Romans: the most important of Paul's many letters and his longest exposition of the deep truths of the Christian faith.

Rome: the 'eternal city'; major centre of Christianity since the arrival there of Peter and Paul; Roman Catholics believe that the Pope is the Bishop of Rome.

Ruth: Old Testament book telling the story of Ruth, ancestor of King David.

S

Samaritans: people of various races who were brought into Samaria to replace the exiled Israelites; regarded as enemies by the Jews, despite coming to worship the God of the Old Testament and holding the Pentateuch as sacred, because of their mixed origins and incomplete religion.

Samson: one of the judges; famed for his physical strength; fought an ongoing battle against the Philistines.

Samuel: Old Testament prophet; last of the judges; chose and anointed Israel's first two kings, Saul and David.

1 and 2 Samuel: books telling the story of Israel from the time of the judges to the end of King Saul's reign, then focussing on King David.

Sanhedrin: ruling council of the Jews in the New Testament period; presided over by the High Priest; had wide powers but was subject to Roman authority; tried Jesus and agreed upon his execution.

Saul: first king of Israel; possibly reigned from 1050 to 1010 BCE, when he was rejected by God and his reign fell apart; succeeded by David.

Sea of Galilee: second largest inland lake in Palestine after the Dead Sea; also known as Chinnereth, Gennesaret and Tiberias.

Second Coming: Christian term for the future return of Jesus.

Septuagint: 'seventy'; Greek translation of the Hebrew scriptures made for those Jews of the Diaspora who did not understand Hebrew.

Sermon on the Mount: collection of Jesus' sayings and parables brought together by Matthew in his Gospel; called the Sermon on the Plain by Luke; contains the Beatitudes and the Lord's Prayer.

Shema: declaration of God's unity; taken from the Jewish scriptures; used as part of the liturgy.

Solomon: David's son and successor as king of Israel, under whom the country enjoyed unparalleled prosperity; reigned from 970 to 930 BCE; responsible for building the first Temple in Jerusalem.

Son of God: title often applied to Jesus in the New Testament; emphasizes the divinity of Jesus.

Son of man: favourite self-description of Jesus; emphasizes his oneness with the human race.

Song of Songs: collection of love poems in the Writings section of the Jewish scriptures; traditionally scribed to Solomon although there is nothing else to connect him with it.

synagogue: 'coming together'; meeting place for the Jewish community; became very important after the Romans destroyed the Jerusalem Temple in 70 CE.

Synoptic Gospels: 'seeing together'; Matthew, Mark and Luke – the three Gospels which take a similar approach to the life of Jesus and have much material in common.

Synoptic problem: puzzle of the relationship between the three Synoptic Gospels.

T

Tabernacle: portable shrine carried by the Israelites in the desert; replaced by the Temple in Jerusalem.

Tabernacles: Jewish autumn festival in which tabernacles or booths are built to remind people of the wanderings of the Israelites in the wilderness; one of three Jewish pilgrimage festivals; also known as *Sukkot*.

Talmud: source of Jewish law; comprises the Mishnah, the Jewish oral law, and the Gemara, the comments of the rabbis from 200 to 500 CE on the Mishnah.

Temple: three successive buildings dedicated to the worship of God that occupied the same site in Jerusalem; Solomon's Temple was the first, built in the 10th century BCE, then destroyed by Nebuchadnezzar in 587 BCE; this was rebuilt by the Jewish exiles returning from Babylonia and completed in 515 BCE, although it lacked the glory of the first Temple; King Herod's ambitious new Temple was begun in 19 BCE, although it was not finished until

64 CE, just six years before it was destroyed by the Romans.

Ten Commandments: ten laws given by God to the Jewish people through Moses; covered an individual's relationship with God and relationships within the community.

1 and 2 Thessalonians: letters of encouragement written by Paul to the church at Thessalonica.

Thomas: one of the 12 disciples; known as Didymus (the twin); doubted that Jesus had risen from the dead.

Timothy: younger colleague of Paul; led the church in Ephesus; was imprisoned for his faith.

1 and 2 Timothy: letters written by Paul to Timothy, his younger colleague.

Titus: letter of Paul to Titus, the young leader of the church at Crete.

Torah: 'law' or 'teaching'; the first and most important of the three divisions of the Jewish scriptures; comprises the five books of Moses: Genesis, Exodus, Leviticus, Numbers and Deuteronomy; also known as the *Chumash*.

William Tyndale: translated the New Testament from Greek into English; due to opposition in England he went to the Continent where he printed his work in 1525; his translation was ceremonially burned in London and in 1536 he was strangled and burned at the stake for heresy.

U

Uzziah: king of Judah from 783 to 742 BCE; also known as Azariah.

V

Vulgate: fourth-century CE translation of the Bible from

Hebrew into Latin by St Jerome; very influential on later English translations.

W

Writings: third division of the Hebrew scriptures, comprising the books of Ruth, 1 and 2 Chronicles, Ezra, Nehemiah, Esther, Job, Psalms, Proverbs, Ecclesiastes, Song of Songs, Lamentations and Daniel.

Y

Yahweh: one of the names given to God in the Jewish scriptures.

Yahwist: one of four original sources for the Pentateuch; here God is given the name 'Yahweh' throughout and most of the colourful stories found in the Torah come from this source; may date from around 950 BCE; referred to by the symbol 'J' in Old Testament source criticism.

Z

Zechariah: late-sixth-century prophet who motivated the Jews to rebuild the Temple in Jerusalem after their exile.

Zedekiah: puppet king of Judah put in place by the Babylonians after the first deportation of the Jews to Babylon; ruled from 597 to 586 BCE.

Zephaniah: Old Testament prophet from the end of the seventh century BCE whose main theme is the Day of the Lord.

Picture Acknowledgments

AKG London: pp. 5 (Coburg Pentateuch [14th century], Add. ms. 19776, fol. 72v: British Library), 23 (Erich Lessing), 68–69 (Coburg Pentateuch [14th century], Add. ms. 19776, fol. 72v: British Library), 70 (Erich Lessing), 86–87 (Erich Lessing), 91 (ms. Add. 11639, fol. 114v: British Library), 114 (Erich Lessing), 137 (*Johann Sebastian Bach* [c. 1720] by Johann Jakob Ihle [1702–74]).

David Alexander: p. 82.

Art Directors & TRIP Photo Library: p. 126 (D. Cole), 142, 148 (H. Rogers), 151 (I. Burgandinov).

Ashmolean Museum/Bodleian Library, Oxford: p. 49.

Julie Baines: pp. 15, 24, 26, 48, 118.

The Bible Society: pp. 124–25, 130 (used with kind permission of The Bible Society).

The Board of Trustees of the Victoria & Albert Museum: p. 28 (*Christ Healing the Sick* [etching] by Rembrandt van Rijn [1606–69]).

Bodleian Library, University of Oxford: pp. 16 (ms. douce 219–20, fol. 182), 17 (ms. douce 131, fol. 96v), 29 (ms. douce 293, fol. 12v), 88 (ms. Junius 11, the Caedmon manuscript, Christ Church, Canterbury [c. 1000], fol. 66), 92 (ms. douce 131, fol. 20), 96 (ms. douce 131, fol. 54), 136 (ms. Eton College 178).

Bridgeman Art Library: pp. 2 (right, Tyndale CXIX, Chapter I of John's Gospel with an illustration of the evangelist writing; text by William Tyndale [c. 1494–1536] [English translator of the Bible], printed in Worms by Peter Schoeffer, from Tyndale New Testament [c. 1525–26]: British Library, London, UK), 3 (left, *The Raising of Jairus' Daughter* [oil on canvas, 1871] by Ilya Efimovich Repin [1844–1930]: State Russian Museum, St Petersburg, Russia), 73 (*Codex Amiatinus*, ms. 1, fol. vr, Ezra writing the sacred books from memory in 458 BCE [frontispiece, seventh century]: Biblioteca Medicea-Laurenziana, Florence, Italy), 76–77 (*The Arab Tale-Teller* [1833] by Emile Jean Horace Vernet [1789–1863]: Wallace Collection, London, UK), 80 (Tyndale CXIX, Chapter I of John's Gospel with an illustration of the evangelist writing; text by William Tyndale [c. 1494–1536] [English translator of the Bible], printed in Worms by Peter Schoeffer, from Tyndale New Testament [c. 1525–26]: British Library, London, UK), 83 (*Martin Luther* by Lucas Cranach the Elder [1472–1553]: National Museum, Stockholm, Sweden), 84 (Charles Darwin [1809–82] [photo] by Julia Margaret Cameron [1815–79]: The Stapleton Collection), 94 (*Isaiah* [detail from the frame of the *Maestà* altarpiece, 1315] [detail of 51591] by Simone Martini [1284–1344]: Palazzo Pubblico, Siena, Italy), 101 (*Judith and Holofernes* [oil on canvas] by Michelangelo Merisi da Caravaggio [1571–1610]: Palazzo Barberini, Rome, Italy), 104–105

(*The Last Judgment* [central panel] by Hieronymus Bosch [c. 1450–1516]: Akademie der Bildenden Künste, Vienna, Austria), 108–109 (*The Raising of Jairus' Daughter* [oil on canvas, 1871] by Ilya Efimovich Repin [1844–1930]: State Russian Museum, St Petersburg, Russia), 113 (ms. Y7 396, fol. 29v, Pentecost, Anglo-Saxon, probably produced at Winchester, for Bishop Ethelwold, later taken to Normandy in the possession of Robert, Archbishop of Rouen, or Robert of Jumiege, Norman Archbishop of Canterbury, who fled in 1052; from the Benedictional of Archbishop Robert [fl. 1037–52]: Bibliothèque Municipale, Rouen, France), 120–21 (*Death on a Pale Horse* [ink and watercolour, c. 1800] by William Blake [1757–1827]: Fitzwilliam Museum, University of Cambridge, UK), 122–23 (*The Finding of Moses by Pharaoh's Daughter* [1904] by Sir Lawrence Alma-Tadema [1836–1912]: private collection), 135 (Sistine Chapel ceiling and lunettes [fresco, 1508–12] [post-restoration] by Michelangelo Buonarroti [1475–1564]: Vatican Museums and Galleries, Vatican City, Italy), 144 (Roy 15 D III, fol. 285, Solomon dictates the Proverbs, *Bible Historiale* [1357]: British Library, London, UK).

The British Museum: pp. 3, 20, 21, 25, 27 (bottom), 31, 78–79, 98–99 (© The British Museum, London).

Susanna Burton: pp. 131, 133, 147.

Stephen Conlin: p. 61.

Hutchison Picture Library: p. 127 (© Titus Moser).

Jon Arnold Images: pp. 8–9, 13, 32, 39, 43, 44, 55, 58, 62, 64–65, 117, 119.

Lion Publishing: pp. 2 (left, both, David Townsend), 4–5, 6–7, 14 (David Townsend), 19 (David Townsend), 27 (top, David Townsend), 40–41, 41, 45 (David Townsend), 50 (both, David Townsend), 51 (David Townsend), 53 (David Townsend), 54, 57 (both, David Townsend), 74, 129.

Maritime Museum, Haifa, Israel: p. 56.

The National Gallery, London: pp. 66–67 (*Saint Jerome Reading in a Landscape* by Giovanni Bellini [c. 1430–1516]), 106–107 (*Christ on the Cross* by Ferdinand-Victor-Eugène Delacroix [1798–1863]), 110–11 (*Christ Driving the Traders from the Temple* by Bernardo Cavallino [1616–56]).

The Oriental Institute of The University of Chicago: p. 10 (courtesy of the Oriental Institute of The University of Chicago).

OMF International: p. 132 (© OMF International).

Performing Arts Library: pp. 138–39 (© Pete Jones/ PAL), 141.

Zev Radovan, Jerusalem: pp. 46, 74–75 (The National Gallery, London, UK).

Robert Harding Picture Library: p. 11.

Sonia Halliday Photographs: pp. 30–31, 84–85.

Derek West: front endpaper, pp. 18, 34–35, 36–37, 38, 42, 52, 59, 93, 97, 103.